'Most of us don't need persuading
and busy and our lives impoverish
Andy Percey, through both a biblic
practical suggestions, examines the
a life-enhancing pattern of rest. If, lik   you are a do-er who
finds rest difficult, you will find it challenging, but in the most
important and helpful of ways.'

Jeannie Kendall – author; co-minister, Carshalton Beeches
Baptist Church; occasional lecturer, Spurgeon's college; and
member, Sutton Street Pastors management board

'The image of the frenzied hamster in the wheel is all too familiar. We know the hamster is tired, but what if, as Andy Percey
suggests, the wheel is also broken? Are we in danger of identify-
ing ourselves by what we do, and losing sight of who we are? Is
there a way to rediscover balance – a way out of the whirlpool
of busyness that so often engulfs us? If these questions resonate
with your experience, this book invites you to make time and
space to rest in the divine spirit at the deep centre of your being.
Grounded in Scripture and peppered with everyday examples,
the book opens up a fresh and potentially transformative understanding of Sabbath time.'

Margaret Silf – author and retreat facilitator

'I loved this book! It totally changed my understanding of the
rest-space God wove into his creation, and of his plan for Sabbath as soul-union time for his people.

'Andy has a great gift for pulling new and rich textures of
meaning from very well-known Scripture. I highly commend
Infused with Life to you.'

Jennifer Rees Larcombe – bereavement and trauma counsellor

'There will be many who welcome this timely book and find their lives restructured because of it. It is biblical, informed, personal, direct and liberating. The fact that it says what it needs to say in relatively brief compass should make it accessible to a multitude. I once heard a former Chief Rabbi claim that the practice of Sabbath is what has enabled the Jewish people to endure so remarkably through time and adversity. For those who wish to complete the race and not just begin it, this book is a wonderful resource.'

Dr Nigel G. Wright – Principal Emeritus,
Spurgeon's College, London

INFUSED with LIFE

Exploring God's Gift of Rest in a World of Busyness

Andy Percey

with every blessing

Authentic

First published 2019 by Authentic Media Limited,
PO Box 6326, Bletchley, Milton Keynes, MK1 9GG
authenticmedia.co.uk

British Library Cataloguing in Publication Data
A catalogue record for this book is available from the British Library.
ISBN: 978-1-78893-065-9
978-1-78893-066-6 (e-book)

Cover design by Roman Tovarnitskyi
Printed and bound by CPI Group (UK) Ltd., Croydon, CR0 4YY

For Bex.

Your beauty and strength have been my inspiration and support, and in you I find and share the best of God.

Thanks

There are many people to say thank you to, without whom no words would have made it to paper.

Becky Fawcett and the staff at Authentic.

Friends at Manvers Street Baptist Church and the wider church in Bath for their support, friendship and prayers.

The staff at Sarum College in Salisbury, for their interest, support and use of their fantastic library for study. They live in a city which is very dear to me, which has been through a difficult time recently. A city that continues to be one of beauty and welcome.

Charlie, Jeannie, Nigel, John and Ian for reading chapters, for sharing their thoughts, and for being so affirming.

My amazing wife, Bex, for her unfailing support, encouragement and belief in me, as well as helping to refine this work. Without you I would not have found the voice to share these words. Thank you for being the one in whom I have seen so much of the best of God's life. Thank you for being my rest, the beautiful person in whom I find life and balance.

Our darling son Leo, for keeping me grounded with what really matters, and for the constant joy you bring to our lives.

Andy Percey

Contents

Foreword

Some people write because they have something to say. Others write because they simply like writing. And then still others write in order to survive. I count Andy Percey in that third category. Andy writes because by writing he can make at least some sense of what is happening in his life: be it tragic loss, as with his first book, or frenetic pace, as with this second, much awaited book.

To be honest, I am surprised he has chosen this theme. Since he moved to the West Country, a few years ago now, I had rather hoped he would have cracked this busyness thing. I had always imagined Somerset to be a rather idyllic place to be a pastor (he says with a wry smile). So the fact that four years into his ministry, he is having to contend for boundaries and proper rhythms, both for himself and for the congregation he serves, tells me, first, how naive I am; second, how widespread modern-day stress has become; and third, how urgent it is to charter a way through.

I had a go at it myself about a decade ago. *The Day is Yours*, written not long after I arrived at Millmead, was my own attempt to create space, using much the same resources as Andy, such as the biblical notion of Sabbath. But as my wife Susanna keeps reminding me, 'It's one thing to write a book but when are you going to do it?' It's a retort I might take up with Andy next time I see him, or maybe Bex, his wife, will do it for me. After all, anyone who can go on a silent retreat as she has done, for forty days on one occasion, is clearly not fazed by so much of the distractedness that Andy writes about here. Like all good marriages, maybe Bex, and their little boy Leo, will be just the accountability Andy will need in order to make sure he not only writes about rest but actually enters it. Actually, I feel sure that he is some way on that path. Not only is Andy a fine writer but, as I was saying earlier, his reason for writing is in order to live it. And from what I know of Andy – both his life and his ministry, as well as his writing of course – one never comes away from time with him feeling harassed or cajoled, but rather, feeling hopeful and energised. The only way I can explain that is because Andy has come from a place of rest.

Revd Dr Ian Stackhouse, Senior Pastor of Millmead, author of *The Day is Yours: Slow Spirituality in a Fast-Moving World*

Preface

As I write these words I am at the end of a three-month sabbatical. For almost twelve years I have served as a pastor in one form or another within the life of the church. It has occupied a great deal of my time, energy and thinking. It has been a great cause of both joy and of sorrow.

Some of my gospel partners in the city have teased me about having a three-month holiday, and I suppose from the outside it could look very much like that. What I can honestly tell you is that exploring rest has been anything but a holiday. It has challenged me deeply; it has corrected me, inspired me and helped to reform me. It has been an experience that at times has been exhausting and at other times has felt as natural as breathing.

Yet after these three months I feel as though I am only just scratching the surface. I feel like I almost need another sabbatical just to come to terms with this one, although I think that my church would need convincing!

As somebody in their early thirties I have grown up in the modern world. We were taught IT at school and were among the first to get mobile phones that could actually fit in your pocket. As a teenager I worked a weekend job and worked on a Sunday. I still do. The world I have grown up in is fast-paced, action-packed and full of soundbites. It never stops. Even though our church has mostly older members, we have a Facebook page and a Twitter account, although who is getting the tweets I could not tell you.

In many ways I feel tired just reading that, but for many years I did not give it a second thought.

It has only been in recent years, and for two main reasons, that I have found this way of being profoundly dissatisfying.

Firstly, through the inspiring example of those around me, especially my wife, Bex. It is through her own personal call to explore God in silence and stillness that I too found a whole new dimension to my faith, and one for which I am incredibly grateful.

Secondly, I came to a period in my life where I came to the end of myself. The old patterns and systems that had been part of my life, to which I had not paid much attention, were no longer working. Far from that, they were failing. Something needed to change.

I needed something different, to experience something deeper, to enter a place of life again.

I heard the ancient call from the prophet Isaiah:

For thus said the Lord God, the Holy One of Israel:
In returning and rest you shall be saved;
in quietness and in trust shall be your strength.[1]

I am aware that being a pastor is not a 'normal job', but it is the one I have and the one from which I share my reflections on my journey. It is my prayerful hope that in the words of this journey you might hear the call yourself, and in hearing it you might return, rest and find strength. In that hope, I offer the following.

1

A Challenging Journey

The hamster may be tired, yes, but it is running on a broken wheel.

It was a rare moment of genuine harmony. Whether it was the sound of the water as it flowed over the rocks, or the light as it danced through the trees, or being there with my wife, Bex, and our son, Leo; something about this moment made me feel connected not only to the world and people around me, but within myself. We were on holiday in the Lake District to celebrate our tenth wedding anniversary, and were having breakfast in a café on the banks of a river that flowed into one of the large lakes. There was nothing overtly spiritual about the activity, but in this moment I experienced a harmony and connectedness that brought me a genuine and deep sense of rest and peace; a moment of Shalom. Have you ever had moments like that?

I have a young family. Leo is almost 3 years old as I begin writing and has yet to develop a pattern of sleep that mirrors what I would even vaguely consider to be 'restful'. Being a parent is a profound joy, and I love my son with every fibre of my being, but parenthood is also an assault on body, mind and spirit, with 'rest' being a word, concept or state that is rarely experienced deeply; you simply grab it when you can.

I am also the pastor of an inner-city church in Bath, with all the demands that full-time pastoral ministry brings.

Moments like the one I experienced in the Lake District that warm July morning happen with far less regularity than I desire or know I need. Much of what I would call 'downtime' becomes more about recovery than this sense of genuine harmony.

What I am trying to say is that I do not write this book as an expert on the subject of rest, nor as one who has found great monastic rhythms to punctuate the busyness of my day. I am writing as a person who is desperately searching for that harmony, and longing to discover a sense of rest which is not elusive but a solid foundation for life.

I am not alone.

A Broken Wheel

The more I speak to people and observe the world around me, the more I become convinced that this is not simply an issue for the 'busy few', but is a pandemic in our modern fast-paced world. I believe that this affects us across every spectrum of our society, young and old, rich and poor; as well as affecting us, body, mind and spirit, as individuals.

Have we forgotten what it is to rest? Have we lost our harmony? It would be too simplistic to say that the blame should be laid at the feet of the worn-out individual, because I believe that our culture itself is to blame. The hamster may be tired, yes, but it is running on a broken wheel.

I have been a pastor for a decade. Part of my role during this time has been to lead churches through change, which is not an easy process. Simply having a desire to embrace the goal you strive for and see it become reality, however important that desire, is only half the story. Very often the process of meaningful change can only happen when we acknowledge that our current methods of reaching that goal simply aren't working. The wheel is broken.

Life can be so full and busy at times, and many of us face moments when everything seems to be happening at once. This is not to say that all these demands are bad. Many of them are good and beneficial and a great blessing to us and those around us, and can give deep meaning and purpose to our lives. At times, though, it feels as though the wheel spins faster and faster and is moving us, rather than us moving it.

Part of the problem I have found in my own life is that so much of my mindset seems to think of rest as 'getting away from it all'; as the proverb says, 'A change is as good as a rest.'

That rest for me becomes a little bit like rehab for the addict. As important as that time is to recover, get straight and clean, there is one very important step that anyone who enters rehab has to make: leaving. You have to re-enter the world. And the brutal truth I have discovered speaking to addicts over the years, is that unless your life in the world is punctuated with patterns and strategies to help you live straight and clean, to stay recovering, then very often relapse is just around the corner. Those who work with recovering addicts will put a great deal of energy and time into making sure that they have all the tools they need to live life fully in the world, avoiding relapse.

For me, the parallel is a striking one. When our expression of rest is simply 'getting away from it all' it might seem to us to be therapeutic or even rehabilitative; but unless it is matched with a life punctuated with rest, then a relapse to those things that caused us to 'get away' is never far off. That is why the wheel is broken, because the rest we often settle for doesn't bring us to a place of everyday harmony with either the world around us or ourselves. It has become a tonic for the weary and the worka-holic, rather than a means to experience a greater degree of life.

A Newer Broken Wheel?

Something needs to change.

Most of us have a sense that we cannot keep running our-selves ragged on the same broken wheel but sometimes are un-sure of how to change, or even what kind of change is needed. So often it is our perceptions that shape our practice, and so it cannot simply be about 'doing things differently', but also a change in heart and mind in the way we think about what rest and work are, and the way they relate to each other as well as the way we relate to them.

In 2016 the initial findings of a massive global study on rest were published in the book *The Restless Compendium*.[1] More than 18,000 people from 134 countries took part in the survey looking at how well we rest and what that looks like in our busy world. The results were very interesting. Broadly speaking, there has not been a great increase in the amount of work we do over the past fifty years. People today still broadly work the same hours as the generation that came before them, but it was recognized that the way we perceive the relationship between work and rest has changed. They helpfully identify part of the challenge for us:

'If someone asks how things are going, many of us tend to answer, "Oh fine, very busy. Bit too busy." This feels true, but of course there's also an element of status in this claim. If you say you are busy, then it implies you are wanted. You are in demand.'[2]

This is something that connects deep within us. The need to be needed and the desire to be wanted connects our work to our worth. It is not to say that this has not always been a challenge but, in the fast-paced world that we live in, these same attitudes that may have in the past spurred us on, are today flooring us.

This has certainly been a challenge for me over the years, because I have often found a certain value and a self-worth in what I do. The logical inference from this is that when I stop doing 'the things I do', so my self-worth diminishes. Within my own ministry this has led to painful times, but it isn't just those in pastoral ministry who can suffer from this problem. A friend and colleague of mine on the chaplaincy team at the University of Bath was a surgeon in a former life. We have spoken on this issue at length and his words very much echo those from *The Restless Compendium*. It seems that there is almost no sector of life where these issues do not touch someone, because we are not just dealing with 'practice' but with the person who is very much tied to what they do.

When we are busy it gives us a sense of value, usefulness and status, and subconsciously rest can feel as though we are letting go of those things. That time spent resting devalues us because it feels as though it is undefined and unmeasured time or, as one person referred to it on a recent BBC Radio 4 programme I heard, 'dead time'.

Perhaps it is these deep-seated ways of seeing ourselves that need to change in order for us to really journey further into rest and experience it more deeply. If all that changes is our practice and not our hearts and minds, then are we simply swapping one broken wheel for another? Simply enjoying an occasional pause in our frenetic movement without anything really changing? Surely there comes a time when what we need is not a newer broken wheel, but to get off all together.

What's Wrong with Everybody Else?

Does any of this resonate with you? Reaching this point has been a journey for me, and one that at times has come with great personal cost because so often in life you learn the most valuable lessons when you get it wrong. It is important to keep ourselves and our own contexts in mind as we engage with the wide-ranging topic of rest.

In stating that this is an endemic problem it is very easy for us to become disconnected from it on a personal level. It would be, and often is, much simpler for us to look at the statistics and at the society around us and point the finger at others. Perhaps this is because we often see and judge in others what we see in ourselves and do not like. It is easier to view the problem as being with everybody else, or with society; it couldn't possibly be me, could it?

In Luke's gospel[3] we see an account of Jesus healing a man who is paralysed and unable to walk. His friends bring him to see Jesus but, on arriving at the house where he is ministering, are unable to get in because of the crowds. At this moment most of us would have either resigned ourselves to a long wait or perhaps the need to come back another day, but not the friends of this man. Instead, they climb the stairs to the roof, and then dismantle it to lower their friend into the middle of the room, right there in front of Jesus. It is a staggering passage of the lengths that love and friendship will go to, but it also has another, perhaps more challenging application for us.

We aren't told anything about the friends who bring this man to Jesus, but what we are told is that their focus is on their friend and making sure he gets into the room. All of these friends were ordinary people just like you and me. They had the same struggles, the same needs, they experienced the same brokenness and need to be made whole. I am sure that they too wanted to meet Jesus, but in this moment the focus was on their friend, and I cannot help but be struck by their selfless act of courageous love and challenged about the lengths I would go to.

We don't know anything about them other than this action, but the challenge I want to draw from this at the beginning of our journey together is: it is very easy to be focused on others, for perfectly good and noble reasons, but as a way of avoiding dealing with issues in our own lives; to identify others as broken and in need of healing – but as a way of avoiding looking deep within and seeing our own brokenness and need for healing. Most of the time we do this without even thinking, and for those of us in Christian ministry we can fall into this trap on a near daily basis. This does not mean that our actions are wrong, but perhaps highlights the complexity of why we 'do what we do'.

Self-awareness is an often underrated trait, but one which enables us in the midst of a busy world to get off the wheel, take a moment and look deep within, focusing on our own lives and the effect that these issues have on us. That is not always easy and requires us to be both bold in our self-searching and gentle with ourselves when we come across what this process throws up.

In his book *Reset*, David Murray looks at living grace-paced lives in a burnout culture. He identifies this issue right at the beginning of his book: 'This is not easy for most of us. We are independent, self-sufficient men [sic] who find it hard to admit weakness, seek help, and change deeply ingrained addictions to overwork, busyness and productivity.'[4]

What has become clear to me in recent years is that this is not just a problem for society, or the church, or the workplace: this is *my* problem and only I can address it with God's help.

I need to go on this journey to discover what rest is really about, otherwise this book simply becomes me preaching freedom from a prison cell. It is a journey I want to invite you to join me on.

Infused with Life

There is a particular coffee shop in Bath where a cup of tea is served with the unusual addition of a digital timer. As I sit waiting to drink my cup of Earl Grey tea the timer is counting down from three minutes thirty seconds because, according to the staff, this is the time it takes for the tea to effectively infuse the water to give you a great cup of tea. As I wait, the tea is going about this process regardless of what is happening around; all it needs is to be in the water and to be given time, slowly infusing its surroundings with delicious flavour.

I wonder if that can be an image for us as we begin the journey. Being infused, not with flavour, but with life.

Jesus said, 'I came that they may have life, and have it abundantly.'[5] I have learned that, for me, the frenetic world of busyness so often does not reflect that abundant life but, rather, robs me of it. Not that there is no life or flavour in busyness at all, but like taking the tea bag out of the water too soon, there just isn't enough time and space for that life to infuse me.

That is what I know I need, to be infused with *his* life, his full and free and abundant life; and I know that nothing else will quite satisfy.

When it comes to the fast-paced world that we now live in, I believe rest is a gift from God. It is not simply a new wheel to run in, but the means through which he infuses us with life: *his* life.

I recently watched a programme, made by BBC Two, called *Pilgrimage*, where seven people living in the public eye walked the famous Camino de Santiago pilgrimage. It was a fascinating programme, and one particular comment stuck with me from it. Towards the end of the journey, one of the participants said that they were not the same people as they were when they had put their first foot down at the beginning. That is my hope in writing this book, and my hope for you in reading it . . . that, come the end, we will not be the same as we are reading this page.

I also want to echo the words of Mark Buchanan in his book *The Rest of God*: 'The world is not dying for another book. But it is dying for the rest of God.'[6]

The journey we are taking together is pilgrimage; a journey of discovering God's gift of rest, of being infused with his life in the ordinariness of our own, and experiencing a balance between work and rest that is not based on recovery but born from a sense of harmony with our Creator and with the world that he has made.

May it resonate deep within us, infuse us and inspire us to live.

2

In the Beginning

In the God of creation, we see the perfect example of one who is in harmony with God's own self. In him there is no conflict between rest and activity, but in both God's rest and activity we see the bursting forth of transformative creativity.

What better place to begin our discussion about rest than at the source or, as it has traditionally been translated, 'In the beginning'.[1]

I wonder whether, like me, you often find yourself disconnected from the words of Scripture? Not that they have lost their importance, but that they have become so familiar to me that they lose a sense of their awesome wonder. I find myself reflecting on this as I read again the words of Genesis 1 and 2. I remember vividly sitting in Sunday school at church when I was a child and colouring in the worksheets and making the collages of the different days of creation. It is worth mentioning that these activities took place almost exclusively indoors and there, I think, is a challenge to our church culture in how it seeks to teach our children and young people about God. I think it was Socrates who said, 'Education is the kindling of a flame, not the filling of a vessel.' So often our church culture seeks to 'fill the vessel' by teaching us knowledge about God and the Bible, but perhaps more flame kindling is needed as we experience more of God. In this instance, getting out there and using the greatest canvas there is to speak more beautifully than any words ever could about the wonderful creativity and beauty of our God.

The challenge for me is that the words of Genesis have become so normalized, almost trivialized, that they seem to be disconnected from my experiences of harmony and awe in creation.

Everything you see around you, and perhaps more profoundly all the things you cannot see, all the rules and laws that govern the cosmos and give shape and meaning to existence as we know it, are not accidental but purposeful. They are spoken into existence by the one whose creative speech not only gives substance to all that is, but meaning too. If we were to stop and allow that to sink in, not to fill the vessel of our minds but to kindle the flames of our imaginations and worship, we would consider again, in awe and wonder, the works his hands have made.

I believe that here we find the first clues in Scripture that will take us on that journey of discovering rest as foundational, because we see it here in the very foundation of the world in which we now live. We cannot remove that foundation without putting at risk the stability of all that we see around us. Perhaps here in Genesis, in the beginning, we can discover it again.

What did the writers of the creation poem mean when they used the phrase 'In the beginning'? This is certainly the beginning of life as we know it, of time, of the cosmos, but surely not the beginning of God. The writers of Scripture affirm time after time that God is eternal: 'LORD, are you not from everlasting?'[2]

It is hard for us to get our heads around concepts like eternity without limiting God to being trapped in our flow of time or completely removed from it. Neither seems an acceptable position to take, and so the early church leaders[3] warned us to stay clear of phrases like 'before the world was made'. After all, time is something that God creates when the sun, moon and stars are made.[4] What we can, and I believe should, affirm is that eternally God is at perfect rest in himself as Father, Son and Holy Spirit; but that, at the same time, could not be more passionately active in himself in the love between Father, Son and Holy Spirit. There is a dynamic stillness in the eternal nature of the Trinitarian God, but that stillness doesn't lead to stagnancy, but rather the bursting forth of creative love.

In the beginning, at the source, we see the one who brings life and consciousness to the cosmos, but in doing so he doesn't just give us the product of his work and the example of his rest: he gives us himself. As J. Philip Newell says: 'The life of creation is a theophany of God. It is a visible expression of the One who is essentially invisible, an intelligible sign of the One who is beyond knowledge.'[5]

Far from simply an account of how things came to be, Genesis is itself a testimony, not simply to the 'beginning' of all created things, but to the truth that all those things find their source in the one who gives himself to that which he has made. That means we need to sit up and take notice as we read these words, because we can find in them not just the story of creation, but beautiful and life-giving glimpses of the Creator.

Chaos and Order

> Then God said, 'Let there be light'; and there was light. And God saw that the light was good; and God separated the light from the darkness. God called the light Day, and the darkness he called Night. And there was evening and there was morning, the first day.[6]

There is a saying that when a butterfly flaps its wings in London there is a hurricane in Sydney, Australia. Little things have a big impact. This is chaos theory, which I have a great deal of sympathy with, because at any given time our house embodies chaos with a certain little person having a big impact on the tidiness of every square foot of our home.

Most of us live our lives with a certain amount of chaos, or at least it feels that way to us. Little things constantly seem to build to big impacts on our lives and wellbeing, and no matter how hard we try, we keep coming back to the same patterns and systems. This struggle between chaos and order is one that is weaved through the words of the creation poem, and one that the early readers of those words would have paid close attention to.

On day one God separates the light and dark, creating night and day. The light that bursts forth into the darkness surrounds the formless and empty earth, but rather than overpowering or consuming it, God gives both their boundaries. This is not a struggle where chaos rules and the winner takes it all, but a process through which God brings his order to the world he creates.

On day three we see God separate the sea and land. The sea, which has so often been the picture of chaos and the unknown to those who have looked offshore in imaginative wonder, is given its boundaries and limits by God. The land, rather than simply having a purpose that is to 'not be the sea', is the place where new life is created: '. . . plants yielding seed, and fruit trees of every kind on earth that bear fruit with the seed in it.'[7]

On day four God creates the sun, moon and stars, only that is not what the writers calls them:

> And God said, 'Let there be lights in the dome of the sky to sep-
> arate the day from the night; and let them be for signs and for
> seasons and for days and years, and let them be lights in the dome
> of the sky to give light upon the earth.' And it was so. God made
> the two great lights – the greater light to rule the day and the lesser
> light to rule the night – and the stars.'[8]

The sun and moon were the objects of worship through much of the ancient world, and still are in some places in our world today. People prayed to them, sacrificed to them and wor-shipped them as divine. Here they are unnamed and regarded as functional because they themselves are not the object of wor-ship, but point to the one who creates them and gives them a purpose – the greater light to govern the day and the lesser light to govern the night.

Order out of chaos is at the heart of Genesis. This is very much foundational to what we are exploring on our journey of rest together. As John Davies puts it well in his book *God at Work*: 'The final goal of all this is not a universe made up from lots of things made out of nothing but a complex harmony of beings brought into reconciliation with each other.'[9]

Darkness and chaos are part of the process of creation. For us as we journey towards a deeper understanding of rest, and as we reflect on the state of our own lives, darkness and chaos will have their own meanings; the writer of the creation poem does not interpret them for us. What is shown, though, is that through the patterns and processes of God's creativity, there can be order and harmony in their place. We can choose to live in the undefined void of chaos, or we can choose to be rooted in the patterns and harmony of God creativity. Creation itself is a witness to those patterns, and we can learn a great deal about how to live in a fast-paced world by reflecting on them.

Patterns and Rhythms

One of the most enjoyable things for me during the winter months is a fire. I love the whole process from start to end, which includes going to get the logs and cutting them down to size to fit the fireplace. Most of the time this process is fairly mechanical and labour intensive, but occasionally I am caught by a beautiful pattern in the wood, and the axe stops (there are actually logs in my wood store that I have not burned because of their beautiful patterns).

Life and faith are full of patterns because creation is full of patterns. In Islam there can be no literal representation of God through art, but what is allowed is pattern.[10] That God can be found in the patterns and the rhythms of his creation seems to be a truth vibrating through the creation poem in Genesis.

One of those patterns is the seasons. Here in the United Kingdom we experience four distinct seasons throughout the year. Winter brings the cold and all around nature seems to be asleep, waiting for the promise of a warmer sunrise. Spring signals the waking of that sleeping world with the bursting forth of new life and endless possibilities. Summer signals that life at its fullest and brightest, with long warm evenings and bright vivid colours and the occasional barbecue. Autumn sees nature winding down again in preparation for the barren period, but a time nonetheless with colour and beauty all of its own. So the years go by as season flows into season and the cycle rolls ever round. Winter gives way to spring, gives way to summer, gives way to autumn, gives way to winter.

This pattern shapes the world we live in and are a part of, but it is a pattern which the Bible encourages us to see within our own lives too. The Teacher gives us this wisdom:

> For everything there is a season, and a time for every matter under heaven:
> a time to be born, and a time to die;
> a time to plant, and a time to pluck up what is planted;
> a time to kill, and a time to heal;
> a time to break down, and a time to build up;
> a time to weep, and a time to laugh;
> a time to mourn, and a time to dance;
> a time to throw away stones, and a time to gather stones together;
> a time to embrace, and a time to refrain from embracing;
> a time to seek, and a time to lose;
> a time to keep, and a time to throw away;
> a time to tear, and a time to sew;
> a time to keep silence, and a time to speak;
> a time to love, and a time to hate;
> a time for war, and a time for peace.[11]

It seems as though most of life's activities can be drawn from the list here in Ecclesiastes chapter 3. However, what is important is not the activities that we find on the list, but the fact that the writer is speaking clearly about different times and seasons in our lives, and that they mirror a pattern in nature that we can learn from.

We tend to want to do it all at once, to multitask. I remember challenging members of a previous church about what they do when they boil the kettle. For most of us this will be time when we simply get on with other jobs, coming back to the kettle when it has boiled and we are ready for our drink to be made. The challenge came in asking people to stand still for the few moments it took for the kettle to boil, to not rush off into other tasks but to simply pause, and then reflect on that rest. Some found it a profoundly irritating experience whilst others found it releasing. Nobody, though, spent the day standing next to the kettle; at some point everyone moved on to the next task because life is not all about the one thing. However, I increasingly feel it is important to be present in each different moment of the day, and not make it about being busy.

According to a website helping children with their homework, 'We have seasons because the earth is tilted (wonky) as it makes its yearly journey around the sun.'[12] Pattern, seasons and balance are words that are becoming increasingly 'wonky' to many in our society who see the aim of life as to pursue the one thing relentlessly until it is achieved; to those still running on the hamster wheel. There is an advert for a well-known cold and flu remedy, where instead of allowing yourself to be ill and rest, we are encouraged to take the medicine and go to work.

We lose the seasons of life at our peril. If we only experience the birthing of things in our lives and never their dying, then space will very quickly run out for new life.

If we only throw away and never keep, then things in our lives will become simply disposable and lack value.

If we spend all our time speaking and never silent, then how will we truly hear those and the world around us?

Does your life reflect the pattern of seasons? Or do you find that you are caught up with the one thing that dominates? Are there activities in your life that you keep doing, even though they fail to bring you life, because they belong in a season that has passed?

Another pattern is sleep. As I mentioned in the previous chapter, our son, Leo, has not yet developed a consistent pattern of sleep and is still not regularly sleeping through the night, which means that neither are Bex and I. All I can tell you about this is that I now understand why sleep deprivation is used as a form of torture, as the many times I have tried to put the plates away in the fridge can attest to that. Sleep is vitally important to the way we function as human beings, and yet we are fairly casual about it. According to recent studies, sleep deprivation is difficult to sustain for more than a few days to a week[13] and that should tell us all we need to know about its importance to us. As human beings we spend around one-third of our lives asleep, meaning that, if we live to 75 years of age, we will have spent 25 years of it asleep – and yet I have never heard a sermon preached on sleep, although several people have fallen asleep during my sermons before! I have rarely in mainstream church heard a prayer prayed about sleep. Every night before Leo goes to bed, we pray with him, and ask God that he will have a good and rested night so he can wake refreshed in the morning to be able to enjoy another day and all it holds. We are not the only animals that sleep; my cat spends a great deal of time perfecting the art.

Do plants sleep? This was the subject of an article in *Popular Science* in March 2014. According to the study, plants have circadian rhythms, which are responsible for when we sleep, wake up and eat; it is our internal body clock. The article says: 'we know that plants use the clock to be able to monitor day length and thus can prepare for seasonal changes (like winter) before the weather actually changes.'[14]

When animals hibernate, they do so as a way of protecting themselves when resources are scarce and they need to conserve energy.

It is clear that God has created the world with a pattern of rest that is essential for all that he has made, whether it be the birds of the air, the trees of the field, the things that creep and crawl on the earth, or human beings. And it seems as you read Genesis chapter 1 that God honours this pattern in his creative artistry. There is a common refrain throughout the first six days: 'And there was evening and there was morning, the . . . day . . .'[15]

There is no record of God's activity during this time. I am not suggesting that God is sleeping, but I am suggesting that God is honouring a creative practice and principle that you cannot give yourself to creative expression until you have given yourself to the rest of the night. If God honours this time, then what is my excuse? I remember all the times that I have stayed up late trying to finish a sermon, or do some other task because it had to be finished. Was I too tired the next day to be able to deliver it faithfully? Would I have been better going to bed and getting up earlier, after a rested night's sleep, to start work afresh? Some of you might be night owls and others, larks. You might work best in the morning or the evening. One is not better than the other, but knowing when you need to rest in a way that refreshes you is key, and sleep plays an important role in that process.

Philip Newell affirms this practice: 'Restoring energies are given to us in the night. In sleep we participate in the way of God . . .'[16]

Like the writer of Genesis, we would be wise to have a pause between evening and morning.

What are your patterns of sleep? Do you give it enough attention? Do you wake feeling refreshed in the morning for another day?

I have an app on my phone that tells me how much sleep I have had the previous night. Some may keep a sleep diary. Periodically it is good to keep track of your sleep patterns, perhaps over the course of a week.

What we see in chapters 1 and 2 of Genesis is that not only did God create the world, but he created it with patterns and rhythms such as seasons and sleep that are there to enhance the life of all things he has created. God has made his creation responsive to the environments around us, and has created us with the ability to change in order to reflect that in any given environment, whether people, animals or plants. In the New Testament, Paul writes to the Corinthians telling them that 'where the Spirit of the Lord is, there is freedom'.[17] We see that Spirit not only at the beginning of creation but playing a role in it, bringing life. Therefore it is right that we say that these patterns do not make us slaves or prisoners to our biology or environments, but we are adaptive and truly free.

It may well be that there are seasons of our lives where we find we are much busier than at others. For example, my friends who work in accounting will tell me that March and April are much busier months than June or July due to the financial end of year. These seasons are the reality of our lives. However, we have been given the freedom, creativity and biology to adapt to those environments in a way that maintains a healthy pattern of rest and activity.

In the God of creation, we see the perfect example of one who is in harmony with God's own self. In him there is no conflict between rest and activity, but in both God's rest and activity we see the bursting forth of transformative creativity.

An interesting example of this in nature is the butterfly.

From a very young age we are aware that the butterfly is born from the caterpillar; that the caterpillar goes on a socially acceptable eating binge, and then finds a spot somewhere and forms a chrysalis. The amazing part of the process is what happens next. Inside the caterpillar are special cells that scientists call 'imaginal cells'. This holds all the future genetic potential that will in time birth into a butterfly. These cells begin to vibrate at a different frequency to the rest of the cells in the caterpillar, and eventually come together to form a new entity, vibrating in harmony together, and the butterfly is born.

Rest can be transformative. On the face of things, there is not a lot happening when you look from the outside of the chrysalis, but from the inside nothing can be further from the truth. The caterpillar needs that environment of rest in order that the transforming activity can take place. There cannot be one without the other; without the rest of the chrysalis, there can be no butterfly, and without the transformative activity of the imaginal cells, then all you have is a caterpillar's tomb. The two go hand in hand in harmony. The challenge for us as human beings is that our work and rest have become disconnected from each other, partly because we have become disconnected from our place in the creation God has made.

A Forgotten Song?

Our family live in the historic city of Bath, which with its Georgian buildings and green spaces is a beautiful city to walk around. Recently I was walking past the Abbey and heard the bells chime for quarter-past the hour to the tune of 'All Things

Bright and Beautiful'. It is a favourite hymn of many in our church, and it is one I remember well from my childhood:

> All things bright and beautiful,
> All creatures great and small.
> All things wise and wonderful,
> The Lord God made them all.[18]

What it reminds me of is that we are all part of this beautiful creation we read about in Genesis; we are connected to each other; and that the vibration of those words that spoke all that is into being buzz, not only through our DNA, but through every atom of every rock, every molecule of air and through every law of every system that makes up the cosmos. The whole cosmos quietly hums the tune of the Creator's voice. Perhaps we are forgetting the tune, or simply it is being drowned out by all the noise of life and the world as we know it.

So where does this disconnect come from? We can find the beginnings of an answer here in Genesis too: 'God blessed them, and God said to them, "Be fruitful and multiply, and fill the earth and subdue it; and have dominion over the fish of the sea and over the birds of the air and over every living thing that moves upon the earth."'[19]

Right here at the beginning of the Bible we come to a passage which, like no other, has shaped the impact we as human beings have had on our world. Often we interpret it in a way that gives us a sense of entitlement, where we can do with the world what we like. We tell ourselves that we are the pinnacle of God's creation, and that rather than being a gift to be treasured, he has given us the world to use as our own.

This is doubly troubling when we couple it with a theology that interprets 'new creation' as implying that 'former creation' has no value.[20] This interpretation often simplifies that theology to mean that the destination of creation as we know it is to be burned up at the end of this age, therefore why should we care about it?

There are two brief comments I would like to make about this before we journey onwards.

Firstly, there is a very present danger when we read the Bible that we take it out of context. What I mean by that in this example is that we take those words in Genesis 1:28, viewing and weighing them on their own without seeking to understand them in the context of the whole creation narrative. We might hear words like 'subdue' and 'have dominion over' here, but if we jump just eighteen short verses, then we get a different picture: 'The LORD God took the man and put him in the Garden of Eden to work it and take care of it.'[21]

The phrase that the NIV translates here as 'work it' the NASB translates 'cultivate it'. There seems to be a world of difference between the two passages, and for that reason alone we need to come back to these discussions and at least be willing to think again about what we see here as our call towards creation.

The second point comes as we look at the context of Genesis 1:28 which we find in the preceding verse:

> So God created humankind in his image,
> in the image of God he created them;
> male and female he created them.[22]

The call to subdue the earth and rule over it comes in the light of being made in the image of God. So we are not to treat the earth as we would like, but we are called to care for the earth in the way that God would care for it; to care for it in a way that mirrors the one who looks upon what he has made and says 'it is good'. When we remove this call to reflect (however poorly) the image of God in the way we subdue, have dominion over, cultivate and care for creation, then we will become separated from knowing who we are or where we are in his world.[23]

It has been important to pause for this discussion on our journey towards a deeper understanding and experience of rest. If we view ourselves as separate from the world which God has made, ruling over it in a way that disconnects us from it, then how can we really be mindful of its seasons? How can we truly benefit from its patterns? How can we really hear the creation song? When we live our theology out like this, then the patterns of rest we see in Genesis become nothing more than off-the-shelf remedies to the ills of life as we want to live it, rather than foundations for the full and free life God has given to us as part of his creation.

As I think about that creation song that we are forgetting, I am reminded of the story I heard about two friends, one from the city and one from the countryside. The friend from the countryside was visiting her friend in the city and the two were taking a walk along a very busy and noisy street. All of a sudden the city-dweller realized that her companion was no longer walking next to her and so turned to see what had happened, and glancing back, noticed her several feel away looking up into a tree. 'What are you doing?' she asked, to which her country friend replied, 'I am listening to the sound of that cricket in the tree.' This is ridiculous, thought the city-dweller, replying, 'There is no way with all this noise you can hear a cricket in that tree.' The country friend smiled, reached into her pocket and took out a £1 coin, held it out in her hand and dropped it. As it reached the ground, everybody within twenty feet turned round and looked. The country-dweller smiled at her city friend, and said softy, 'I suppose it depends what you tune your ear to hear.'

Shelly Miller sums it up beautifully: 'Rhythms of rest are possible because they were there from the beginning.'[24]

As we journey forwards, will we tune our ears to hear the song of our Creator God through his creation? Will we wonder at the seasons and reflect on how they can shape the seasons of our own lives? Will we see the patterns and rhythms of rest and allow them to inspire and shape our own? Rather than setting ourselves above this creation, will we root ourselves in it, and begin to learn to sing again the song that all creation has been singing since the beginning?

3

The God Who Rests

Rest is about a holistic harmony that allows us to be who we were made to be, because it is an expression of who God is.

Having looked at what we can learn from the rhythms and patterns of creation in Genesis, we move on to explore perhaps the greatest case for the importance of rest in the Bible. God rests!

Thus the heavens and the earth were finished, and all their multitude. And on the seventh day God finished the work that he had done, and he rested on the seventh day from all the work that he had done. So God blessed the seventh day and hallowed it, because on it God rested from all the work that he had done in creation.[1]

In the spring before Leo was born, we took a family trip to North Yorkshire where my mum's side of the family originates from. There were twelve of us in total – my parents, aunts and uncles, my grandmother, my sister with her family and Bex and I. We began the holiday one down, though, as my brother-in-law, Fraser, was running the London Marathon on the Sunday, clocking in a very respectable six hours and fifty minutes. Not only did he complete the Marathon, but he drove from London to North Yorkshire that same evening, clocking around 230 miles of driving to add to the twenty-six he had already run.

The next day we went to Fountains Abbey where Fraser, now feeling the miles from the previous day a little bit more acutely, needed to be pushed around the Abbey in a wheelchair. His body had reached the point where he had to stop and rest!

Surely God wasn't worn out? The prophet Isaiah said:

The LORD is the everlasting God,
the Creator of the ends of the earth.
He does not faint or grow weary . . .[2]

If God does not grow faint or weary and wasn't being pushed around the Garden of Eden in a wheelchair, then there must be something more intentional going on here. God doesn't need to rest, so why does he?

A Place for God to Rest

The more I read Genesis chapters 1 and 2, the more I cannot escape the reality that part of God's creative activity is to create a space to rest. The question of why God might go to all those lengths to create a space to rest when he does not need to might whirl endlessly round in our minds unless we understand something different about rest.

When many of us think of rest, we think of it as a means of relaxation, not dead time but certainly downtime. However, according to John Walton in his commentary on Genesis, what we see here in God's resting in Genesis chapter 2 goes far deeper than that: 'Rest does not imply relaxation but more like achieving equilibrium and stability.'[3]

We tend to see the world in black and white; in either/or language; to talk about equilibrium and stability in God would, by very nature, imply the possibility that God can be instable and imbalanced. If this is true, then creation becomes almost cathartic for him, and his rest becomes a sort of divine self-soothing after the rigours of creative activity.

God is fully who God is eternally. If our early church parents rightly told us that there is no attribute which God does not have eternally, or rather, who God is God is always, then this stability and equilibrium must have a more than simply black and white interpretation.

Scripture tells us that 'God is love'.[4] There has never been a more profound and world-changing statement about the divine nature than this. Love is not simply what God does but is who God is eternally and fully. That love is perfectly expressed in and between Father, Son and Holy Spirit, but that love is not limited. This love is an expression and giving of 'self' to the other, between the different persons of the Trinity. It is also a giving of God's self to the other, to that which is not God, where the love that is in very nature who God is spills out in beautiful expressiveness and creativity. This act of self-giving love becomes in that moment creative. When a child is conceived in, and as a self-giving expression of, the love of their parents, then we get a glimpse of what this creativity is like.

So what does this rest on the seventh day signify? When viewed in this light, it can be seen as an expression of the completion of that act of self-giving love flowing from within the very being of God, not that he has now achieved equilibrium and stability that he did not have before. It is here that he infuses us with his creating life.

The seventh day is a pause, a moment to breathe and for all creation to reflect back to God the love that has birthed it. It is a holy moment rooted deep which ties creation and Creator together, not in activity, but in being – that simply put, in this moment, creation is what it is, we are what we are, because God is who he is.

When we rest, it is firstly and most profoundly much more than simply a pause from our activity; a space. It is an exclamation mark which exclaims who we are on a deep level, children of a Creator God. It is an exclamation that causes John to exclaim 'that is what we are'![5]

Rest is about a holistic harmony that allows us to be who we were made to be, because it is an expression of who God is. It is not simply finding harmony within, or finding harmony with or in creation, but in a very real sense entering in to the very harmony of God expressed so beautifully in all he has made. In that we find who we really are.

A Space for God to Enjoy

There is another dimension to God's rest, which is that creation is a space for God to enjoy.

If we look back though Genesis chapter 1, then we find not only the account of the way God has created, but we see this poem punctuated with pauses where God takes a step back and enjoys what he has made, calling it 'good'.[6] Then at the culmination of his work at the end of the sixth day we read: 'God saw everything that he had made, and indeed, it was very good.'[7]

God delighted in what he had made, and therefore it would seem perfectly in keeping with what we have seen in days one to six to say that God's rest on the seventh day was a means through which he could enjoy his creation. We see glimpses of this throughout the psalms, most noticeably in Psalm 104:

> May the glory of the LORD endure for ever;
> may the LORD rejoice in his works . . . [8]

Many years ago I worked for one of the high street banks and I remember clearly a friend advising me about getting a good work/life balance. His advice took the form of the phrase: 'You should work to live, not live to work.' The view seems sound enough. If our whole expression of life becomes about work, however enjoyable our work can be, but we fail to cultivate the space to live beyond it, then our lives can become one-dimensional. There have been times in ministry when that balance has been wrong for me, where I have spent too much time without boundaries to the point where the work I was doing took over all else. It is important to say that for me those times, left unchecked, have led to some of the darkest moments in my life. I remember speaking to a good friend in recent years whose life was dominated by work in the hope that he could achieve all he wanted to as quickly as possible, and then he would have time to enjoy all the things that mattered: family, friends, health, rest. The problem for him was that as a result of this one-dimensional living, his family, friends and health were suffering and he found that rest was simply a matter of recovering to nose back to the grindstone. Happily my friend had noticed these patterns and was able to put in place healthier and more life-giving ones.

Not only does this way of life, 'creativity without rest, and productivity without renewal, lead to the exhaustion of inner resources'[9] but it falls woefully short, by any measure, of the full and free life that the Father offers us abundantly in Christ through the Spirit. This is why God's enjoyment of his creation in his rest is such a helpful example to us. Angela Tilby speaks into this conversation: 'The seventh day is sacred time, playtime and the heart of time. It is key because it is about completion. Work, then, for God, is not an end in itself.'[10]

That work is not an end in itself for God is a challenge to the work ethic of the society that we live in, but at times our Christian theology has been far from willing to hear this challenge. In the twentieth century the phrase 'the Protestant Work Ethic'[11] was coined, expressing a theology dating back to the Reformation about work as a sign of grace. When coupled with the apostle James telling us that 'faith without works is . . . dead',[12] what can arise is a drivenness to keep working as a means of expressing God's grace in your life. 'If you want to show more grace just work harder' might seem like a crude interpretation of this concept, but in pastoral ministry as well as in life in general, I have come across so many people whose expression of work falls into just such a category. People with a vocational work fall into this trap especially easily, although for anyone who finds their value and worth in what they do, it can be particularly troubling. This view of work is expressed from a very young age where children are told that 'the devil finds works for idle hands', which seems to imply that work or activity are somehow more God-ordained. More worryingly, are we really saying in phrases like this to our children that rest or 'idleness' are somehow evil?

Working hard is important, and we will come on to explore that a little more in later chapters. What I am saying is that we have got the balance wrong, and in order to redress that imbalance we need to look again at rest not only as something God

has ordained but as something God enjoys. John Davies puts it
well, that 'the seventh day tells us that rest is good in itself'.[13]

Then God blessed the seventh day and made it holy . . .[14]

There are three blessings we see in the creation poem, two in
Genesis chapter 1 and the other at the beginning of chapter 2.
God blesses the living creatures on the fifth day;[15] he blesses
the first human beings on the sixth day;[16] and God blesses the
seventh day.[17] What makes this seventh day, the day of rest,
different to the other days is that God not only blesses it but he
makes it holy because it is a day when he rests. Perhaps then we
can say that within an overall pattern of work and rest, work is
blessed by God but rest is sanctified.

Is It Good?

God delights in his creation, stepping back to enjoy and be in
harmony with all that he has made, but how many of us will
wait until a crisis hits before we step back and look at what is
going on in our lives?

Not only is the seventh day the supreme stepping back to enjoy
the 'very good' world that he has made, but throughout Genesis
chapter 1 we see God stepping back seven times to say 'it is good'.[18]

There is something significant in this when it comes to rest.
It is almost as though each of these moments are little pauses
in the creative process, little moments of rest that allow God to
celebrate and enjoy what he has made, as he works. The epic
culmination of this is of course the seventh day, when the work
is completed, but here we get these little forerunners to it. It
saturates all of creation with these moments of divine pause

and celebration, radiating out from all that is and is mirrored in our doing likewise, in pausing and celebrating in the midst of our lives too. This is celebrating God's rest. Not just one epic rest at the end of the week, but the spirit of creative pause and celebration in the midst of it.

The question this poses for me is: how can I really appreciate what I do as work if I do not allow myself time to step back and enjoy it, to celebrate it? There is a sticky note program on my desktop screen where I write all the things I need to get done in the coming week. On Monday morning I plan the week and put the list in an order of priority. Over the course of the week I delete the items on the list until, hopefully, by the end of the week the list is empty. Then the cycle repeats itself at the start of another week. What I am challenged by as I read of these mini-pauses in Genesis 1, is that I do not take any time, even a brief moment after an item is removed, to step back and evaluate. Was that good? Was it very good? Or like my school report, 'could do better'? Do I give space for these moments of pause and celebration in my working week? Because these mini-pauses in some way enrich the ultimate rest, because you have a sense in which work is completed, valued and allowed then to be what it is. Otherwise this is what the main rest becomes, thinking back over the week and evaluating, which really robs you of the mental rest that is so important.

It Is Finished

I want to end this chapter by reflecting on, appropriately, 'completion'.

That is what we see on the seventh day when God rests from the work he has done. If we look again at Genesis 2:1,2 then we see how emphatically the writer wants to stress that this work is completed: 'Thus the heavens and the earth were *finished*, and all their multitude. And on the seventh day God *finished* the work that he had *done*, and he rested on the seventh day from all the work that he had *done*' (emphases mine).

It is interesting in this sense that God does not bless any of the previous six days. He blesses the creatures he has made, but he does not bless the working day. He does bless the seventh day because this is the day when he stops. Why then do we not say that God made the world in six days and then rested for a day? German theologian Jürgen Moltmann explains: 'In what does the completion of creation consist? It consists in God's rest. It is a completion through rest.'[19]

This is a particular challenge to me because so much of the work that I do seems unfinished and ongoing. Whether it is pastoral work, or vision casting, or managing change, it often feels as though there is no end product, and with no end product it is hard to feel that something is finished. One of the things I like doing when I have the time, and which I am reasonably good at, is baking. I have not yet got to the level of being able to cook food generally, unless on the barbecue, but making a cake is something I do enjoy doing, in no small part because it gives me an end product. I weigh and mix the ingredients, put the mixture in the oven and wait. In time, the cake is ready and, once it has cooled, we can enjoy it with a cup of tea or coffee. I do not need to do anything else to it, it is finished. As you read the Genesis poem, you get the feeling that in some tiny way this is part of God's creative process. He has spoken and it has become, and then he takes a step back to see the finished product. There is nothing else in that moment that is needed. Angela Tilby reminds us that God 'is not so anxious about the universe that he needs to be doing things to it all the time'.[20] This work of creation is finished.

It is also helpful for us to think about the word that has been translated as 'rested'. Whilst there are several possible translations of the word (which is not uncommon in Hebrew translation), the one which seems most appropriate, and which most scholars agree on, is that he 'desisted from his work'.[21] This is what rest looked like for God on the seventh day: no work. It leads leading Hebrew scholar Robert Alter to translate the verse like this: 'And God completed on the seventh day the task He had done, and he ceased on the seventh day from all the task He had done.'[22]

Does my definition of rest translate as 'cease from all the task'? To stop, no work? And yet this seems to be the challenge here in Genesis chapter 2. That not only has God created a world that beats to a rhythm of rest and activity, but God chooses to honour that beating in his own rhythm. In that sense these patterns and rhythms, the harmony we see in creation, are a constant reflecting of the image of the Creator by his creation, and a reflecting of creation's goodness back to it by the Creator.

What we see here in Genesis 2 is profound. It is profound because this space created by God's ceasing of work, his resting, is as passionate an expression of his love as what we see on the first six days. It creates a space for relationship to exist, a space to be, not only for creation but for God himself to join them in it.

And in that sense God's stillness here is still deeply creative. This is why we talk about the world being made in seven days and not six, because what happens here on the seventh day is as profoundly creative as what has come before.

It is this rest that sets the rhythm of creation, and it is this rest that sets the tone for our ongoing discussion . . . Sabbath!

4

Receiving Sabbath

Sabbath is the means through which we are reconnected to each other and the world. It is the gift of a community that continually rebalances to be in line with the needs of the other, reflecting the very heart of Creator God.

Having looked at the beautiful and diverse expression of rest within the Genesis poem, and having seen how God imaginatively weaves into that creation a space to enjoy all he has made, and how it is infused with his life, we now come to look at how God's people received this rest in the gift of Sabbath. In making this transition from the colour of creation to the grey of the stone tablets of the Ten Commandments, there is a small sense in which we are moving into something far more restrictive and legalistic than we have come from. That is how the law is often conveyed, as black and white, colourless, impinging on the freedom and grace of living faith. To believe that is to misunderstand what the law is about, so before we look at the specifics of the Sabbath command, it is important to recalibrate what the commands themselves are really about.

Firstly, we must understand what it is that we usually mean when we use the word 'law'. We often view the law we see given in Exodus in the same way we view the law of the land. It is there to stop us from doing things that are harmful to society, with penalties for breaking those laws deterring us from doing so. One of the historical arguments in favour of capital punishment has often been that the populous would be so frightened of the consequences that they would not commit the worst crimes. So often this is how we view the Ten Commandments; break them and receive the spiritual equivalent of capital punishment. When viewed in this light it is easy to see how grace seems to fly in the face of the law, a world of colour surpassing the cold, hard grey of the stone tablets. When viewed in this light, the law does not seem like a gift. It is at best an obligation to be observed either from a sense of fear or religiosity. Let me put it another way: have you ever received a gift from someone who made you feel, by the way they offered it, that receiving that gift was a burden? That even though you might have wanted it, maybe even needed it, it was tainted slightly because they gave it in a way that made it feel like an imposition or a burden? If you can associate with that analogy then you will appreciate that it doesn't feel much like a gift. If we view the law, the commandments, as though they were offered to us as a burden, as something to be imposed on us, then they will not feel like much of a gift either.

I do not believe we should understand the law this way. The word 'Torah', which we often translate as 'law', would better be thought of in terms of instruction or teaching; or to take the word back to its roots: *pointing the way*.

When Jesus refers to himself as 'the way',[1] would those who listened have seen flickers of the language of Torah? Jesus after all says that he has come not to destroy the law but to fulfil it,[2] to be the one who ultimately points and clears the way to God.

The Jewish scholar and theologian Abraham Heschel put it like this: 'It is for the law to clear the path, it is for the soul to sense the Spirit.'[3]

It is not that the law is purposeless for a New Testament people, but that the law was always a forerunner for the one who would come later, like John the Baptist carved into tablets of stone, preparing and pointing the way for the grace that was to come.

If we view the law given through the Ten Commandments in this light, as the pointing of the way to the God of creation in a busy and cluttered world, ultimately finding its fulfilment in Jesus, then we see this Sabbath not simply as an obligation to be adhered to, but as a gift to be received on the journey.

> Remember the sabbath day, and keep it holy. Six days you shall labour and do all your work. But the seventh day is a sabbath to the LORD your God; you shall not do any work – you, your son or your daughter, your male or female slave, your livestock, or the alien resident in your towns. For in six days the LORD made heaven and earth, the sea, and all that is in them, but rested the seventh day; therefore the LORD blessed the sabbath day and consecrated it.[4]

I find it really interesting that more words are given to this, the fourth commandment, than to any of the other nine, with almost one-third of the content of the commands speaking about the Sabbath. Even so, as we reflect honestly about our own patterns of rest, we must admit that, despite its importance, this commandment is the one that we are most likely to break. Perhaps that is the very reason why so much of the content of the commandments is devoted to keeping Sabbath.

'Remember the sabbath day, and keep it holy.'

My nana, who is 95 as I write this chapter, has dementia. I am grateful that it has not changed her personality a great deal, but her memory is what has suffered the most, as well as her ability to piece together the parts of what she can remember. When I see her I often wrestle with whether to explain to her who I am, knowing that she will have forgotten in ten minutes' time, or whether to be just another friendly visitor. Amongst all the rich memories of her long life, people and places, joys and sorrows, specifics can get lost: she just doesn't remember.

When we are called to remember the Sabbath, it is not like our simple human remembering. It is more than just a recalling of events past, or piecing together the rich tapestry of the life of faith. If so, then we know all too well that we will have forgotten in a few minutes' time when some distraction or another causes our minds to wander. This remembering requires something of us. Many of the commentary writers[5] draw our attention to God's response to his people's suffering as slaves in Egypt: 'God heard their groaning, and God *remembered* his covenant with Abraham, Isaac, and Jacob.'[6]

This remembering for God was not a nostalgic and familiar mental tug, it was a deep stirring which resulted in action, an action that led to freedom and life for his people. In much the same way for us this remembering of the Sabbath requires an action, and one which will lead to freedom and greater life for us and for the creation of which we are a part.

The law was not introducing the people to something that was new. They had grown up with the retelling of the stories of Creator God, and they were already familiar with the concept of Sabbath before the giving of the law at Sinai. In Exodus 16 we read about how God sends manna to feed his people, telling them to gather up the food in advance of the seventh day's start because that day 'is a day of solemn rest, a holy sabbath to the LORD'.[7]

But through receiving Sabbath in the law, this commandment was more than an occasional moment but was to be a framework for their personal and common life.

The year before I started training for ministry, I met on a regular basis with the pastor of our church. Even now, more than a decade later, I am grateful for those times with Dave, and much of what we talked about I can still remember well. He suggested working through a book by Gordon MacDonald called *Ordering Your Private World*.[8] The book explores how in our busy and fast-paced culture, we need to cultivate space in order to live from a place of spiritual balance. Dave knew me well enough to know that this is where I needed challenge as a young man of 22 – discipline. The reality of this struggle is one that many of us can relate to. We find it hard to be disciplined, and left to our own devices and bombarded by the constant distraction of modern living we would find it hard to cultivate this space. So God in his wisdom has not only provided us with the gift of this space in Sabbath, but has provided it within a framework that shapes our common life and draws us back to it week after week.

What does the call to keep this time holy mean considering that we have already seen in Genesis 2 that it is God who inaugurated the holiness of this day? An often-used definition of holiness is 'set apart for the LORD', and here we find the first glimpses that this day is to be different because God's people are called to set this day apart for the Lord. The people of God found themselves living in a world where this set-apart day of rest was not only rare, but often scorned by the cultures around them. It would have been easy to slip back into practices and work ethics of cultures that were more dominant, or even more familiar to a people recently freed from the relentlessness of slavery. This gift of rest to his people was a holy gift of time set apart for a set-apart people.

We find it easy to slip into dominant work ethics. We live in a culture where work is the end in itself, and in order to achieve the things that matter to this world – money, status, power etc. – one must work all the hours God sends in order to achieve them. Sabbath is about remembering that these hours God has sent are to be set apart for something different, for him, rather than running on the ever-turning wheel of our culture's work ethic. The purpose of Sabbath is not recovery but holiness as Heschel says when quoting The Zohar:[9] 'The Sabbath is not for the sake of the weekdays, the weekdays are for the sake of the Sabbath. It is not an interlude but the climax of living.'

Wholeness.

But the seventh day is a sabbath to the LORD your God; you shall not do any work – you, your son or your daughter, your male or female slave, your livestock, or the alien resident in your towns.[10]

As we have seen in the creation poem, we live in a world that is interconnected. The life of the Creator is found in all things, flowing through the very fabric of the cosmos. We have seen how one of the very first calls on human beings was to reflect the image of God in caring for the world that he had made. That call was not just for the gardeners of early Genesis but is a call through them to humanity as a whole in every time and place, and it is a call that we need to hear with fresh ears, today especially. That perhaps is a subject for another book!

The law was given not just to bless God's people, but so that God's people may be a blessing to the world. Sabbath is the same. It is not just given to us for our good alone, but so that we too may be a blessing to the world around us. It is easy to forget this. When I was in Sunday school, we were asked to try to memorize the Ten Commandments. In order to do that, the slightly longer ones were simplified in order to help in the task. So the Sabbath command was shortened to simply: 'Remember the Sabbath and keep it holy.' On the one hand, I can totally understand that asking children to remember the whole text is challenging. However, the greater challenge comes, I think, in disconnecting the opening part of the command with what follows. Because this commandment not only tells us what God is asking of his people, but it tells us why and what that looks like. Without the rest of the text, then Sabbath is open simply to my own interpretation of what I need.

When Sabbath becomes simply about me, then like in so many other ways, it is my relationships that suffer. I am connected to the people and the world around me. I have found in my own life that when I fail to rest, when I fail to honour the Sabbath rhythms as holy, then it affects those around me too. I am tired and less present, I am irritable and less caring, I tend to put a heavier burden on others rather than seeking to protect and be a blessing to them. My tiredness has an impact on creation too. I may not have any livestock, but I do own a car, and when I am exhausted, I tend to drive more which releases more CO_2 into the atmosphere than would have been the case if I had been rested enough to walk.

God does not only bless me with the Sabbath, but so that I might be a blessing to others.

Slavery has long been abolished in the United Kingdom, but what does this word have to say to business owners in the way they treat their staff? Do we make sure that our workers have the space and rest to really live? What about churches? Do we make sure that ministers and other staff members are getting at least one uninterrupted day off a week where we do not expect any work from them?

Whilst I do not own livestock, what about those in the farming industry who do? Or those who work in professions and industries where animals do work? Are we making sure that animals get the rest that they need so that on the Sabbath they can rest?[11]

Sabbath is the means through which we are reconnected to each other and the world. It is the gift of a community that continually rebalances to be in line with the needs of the other, reflecting the very heart of Creator God. As Heschel beautifully describes:

> The Sabbath, thus, is more than an armistice, more than an interlude; it is a profound conscious harmony of man and the world ... All that is divine in the world is brought into union with God. This is Sabbath, and the true happiness of the universe.[12]

Are there people in your life who would benefit from you receiving the gift of Sabbath?

Relationships which could be strengthened? Workers and creatures that can be honoured?

Then there is the call to do no work. It is a challenge to define what work is in a time where there are so many different definitions. Even within the Jewish faith there has been much debate over many centuries as to how to come to an adequate definition of work or, to use the word in Torah, '*Melakhah*'. A definition which links with what we have seen in Genesis is to do with human dominance over creation. The general principle behind it is that God has created human beings with intelligence and creativity through which we can bring nature under control. What this can do is both disconnect us from being part of that creation, but also leads us to a degree of self-reliance which hinders our dependence on God.

According to Grunfeld, the definition of *Melakhah* (work) is: 'An act that shows man's mastery over the world by the constructive exercise of his intelligence and skill.'[13]

This definition is broken down into thirty-nine categories which for Jews constitute the forbidden work on the Sabbath. We will explore the relationship between work and rest a little bit more deeply in a later chapter.

But the Sabbath is more than simple cessation of work, it is the laying down of those things before God. Towards the conclusion of Psalm 46 we read these well-known words: 'Be still, and know that I am God!'[14]

However, the word we commonly translate as 'be still' is perhaps better and more challengingly translated 'let go'.[15] 'Let go, and know that I am God.'

What does the word 'work' mean for you? If Sabbath is a holy gift, what are you being called to lay down or cease from doing in order to enter it? 'He who wants to enter the holiness of the day must first lay down the profanity of clattering commerce, of being yoked to toil.'[16]

As you journey into Sabbath in search of knowing the one in whom 'we live and move and have our being'[17] more deeply, what does he call you to let go of?

For in six days the LORD made heaven and earth, the sea, and all that is in them, but rested the seventh day; therefore the LORD blessed the Sabbath day and consecrated it.[18]

I remember singing the song 'This is the Day' in church when I was a child. I often came away with the impression that the song was to thank God for Sunday, which was a special day when we gathered together as his people. Over years my views have changed, and I firmly believe that we can, on any given day, say along with the psalmist, 'This is the day that the LORD has made'.[19] However, as I look at God's blessing and hallowing of the seventh day in Genesis, and the reminder of it here at the giving of the law, I do feel a sense of the separateness of the Sabbath day. As we have already affirmed, this is not like any other day, or at least it is not supposed to be.

Here, though, at the end of the commandment we are drawn back again to the story of Genesis where we have journeyed from. God of wondrous creative activity, creates, rests and blesses that day making it holy.

We have already seen holiness described as a setting apart for God, but there is another definition of holiness that we see here, which is to reflect the holiness of God. Several times in Leviticus God says to his people: 'You shall be holy, for I the LORD your God am holy.'[20]

God has acted in holiness in consecrating the seventh day, and for God that holiness came in the shape of rest. To respond to the holiness of God, for his people, was to reflect that holiness in remembering and keeping the Sabbath.

There has been some debate as to whether the call is here to simply cease from work with no implication of rest, or whether the two go hand in hand. When we look at the text in Genesis 2:2,3, what we see mentioned in the Hebrew are God's finishing of his work and his ceasing from it, with rest not being implied. However, when we come to the commandment here in Exodus the word 'rest' features much more prominently, not only to describe God's cessation from work on the seventh day, but also the response of his people in receiving, remembering and keeping the day. This is picked up in the NRSV translation of the Bible I am using in this book, with both passages using the word 'rested'. Patrick Miller finds the same conclusion in his book on the Ten Commandments: 'As both the commandment rationale and the Genesis creation conclusion make clear, it is only in the light of God having stopped work and rested that the Sabbath day is blessed and sanctified.'[21]

Seeing God's holy rest on the seventh day, how else can his people respond other than to do the same?

There is another dimension to this rest which is not picked up on here in Exodus but is in the mirror to this passage in Deuteronomy 5:

> Observe the sabbath day and keep it holy, as the LORD your God commanded you. For six days you shall labour and do all your work. But the seventh day is a sabbath to the LORD your God; you shall not do any work – you, or your son or your daughter, or your male or female slave, or your ox or your donkey, or any of your livestock, or the resident alien in your towns, so that your male and female slave may rest as well as you.[22]

These first three verses of the commandment in Deuteronomy are almost identical to those we have already studied in the Exodus account. The difference comes in the following and final verse of the commandment:

Remember that you were a slave in the land of Egypt, and the LORD your God brought you out from there with a mighty hand and an outstretched arm; therefore the LORD your God commanded you to keep the sabbath day.[23]

Here there is no mention of God's rest, but instead a direct link to the history of his people.

Whatever we imagine the slavery of God's people in Egypt to be, the reality must have been far worse. It always is. Work would have been back-breaking, unbearably long, with no rest. Much like Rome, Egypt wasn't built in a day, but it was built in a hurry because the pharaohs who commissioned the work were working to a clock, their own body clocks. They wanted to see the monuments that they were building, or rather that were being built on the backs of slaves. When you do not care about your workforce, and the workers are expendable, why trouble yourself with giving them rest? The times may have changed, but this attitude is still as prevalent in our world today as it ever has been. There are many who work in the sweat shops of our Western industries, hidden away in often appalling conditions to feed the almost insatiable desire of 'their masters'.

We see this when Moses first goes to Pharaoh in Exodus chapter 5 and asks for the people to be given time to stop work and worship God. We see pharaoh's reply in verse 4: 'Moses and Aaron, why are you taking the people away from their work? Get to your labors!'

Not only does he not give them leave from their work, but for even asking he forces them to gather their own straw to make bricks rather than provide it for them; he makes their work harder.

This level of work was the reality for God's people, generation after generation for centuries. Countless died. Generations were born who knew nothing but this life, and had to raise their children in it.

Despite their sudden and unexpected freedom, the scars of slavery run deep in the soul as well as the skin. Then they come to the mountain and they hear the commandments and the fourth commandment to rest. I cannot begin to imagine what hearing this commandment would have meant to these people.

This commandment, though, is far more than a divine attempt to redress the pains of slavery on his people. It says something profound to the soul as well as the body. In Egypt, work was not only their seamlessly unending task, it was what defined them. It was their purpose as well as their task. It was bound up in the very fabric of who they were, and their survival depended on their ability to keep working. Now they had been freed not only from the physical existence of slavery, but from the identity of slaves. No longer was their identity to be found in their work alone, and the best remedy for this was to stop working and rest. And rest to the work-weary slave is medicine for the soul as well as the body.

And whilst, unlike in Egypt, the body could recover through receiving this gift of Sabbath, Heschel rightly describes Sabbath as 'a day for the sake of life'.[24] Here they were to be infused with the life of God, a life full of the vibrancy of creation, a life mirroring the life of God, a life defined not as slaves but as God's very own people.

Are there times when it feels as though you have become a slave to work? I know that there have been moments like this in my life, where it wasn't only the balance that was wrong but my identity. I got too wrapped up in believing that I was what I did. Whilst that is in so many ways incomparable to the slavery experienced by God's people in Egypt, or by the countless slaves around our world today, it still leaves scars on the soul.

Do you see those scars in your life? Has your pattern of work come at a cost?

Sabbath rest is not only a time and space for those scars to heal, it is the space through which we receive the one thing that can heal them, the life of God himself; a God of freedom, love, grace and wholeness. A father who loves to give good gifts to his children.

He offers this gift to his people through Sabbath, every single week. Like any gift, though, you have to receive it, and that is the challenge for each of us moving forwards.

5

Living Sabbath

Sabbath is a time to rediscover our place in the world, to reconnect and to bask in the warmth of relationship.

Several years ago I was asked to lead a men's prayer breakfast, looking at this commandment to remember and keep the Sabbath as part of a wider series informally exploring the commandments. We explored some of what we have looked at already, and then we spoke about our individual experiences of keeping, and failing to keep, Sabbath and what we could draw from that to encourage each other. What struck me in particular was that in this wide group of men containing accountants and plasterers, doctors and lighting designers, encompassing a wide range of ages and backgrounds, many if not all struggled to find regular patterns of rest in their lives. Not only did they struggle to find it, but many knew that they were struggling as a result. The challenge that presents itself to us on a daily basis is that it is one thing to receive Sabbath, but something entirely different to live it.

When Bex and I buy Leo a present, what delights us as much as seeing his face when he receives it is when we can see him playing with that present or using it and it bringing joy to his life. I remember one Christmas we bought him a play kitchen which meant I had to stay up late working through the instructions and putting it together so that when he came down in the morning it would be ready for him. It was wonderful to see him discover it, and to delight in it. Here we are eighteen months later and he still plays with it and it still brings him delight, and that is a different kind of joy.

In a far fuller and greater way, is that how God feels towards us as his children? That there is a joy in us discovering and receiving the gift he has given to us in Sabbath rest, but a different but equally full joy in seeing it become a means of delight that punctuates our lives?

We often need to be proactive in crafting out time and space, because the world does not stop just because we have decided to. All the demands that we face, all the pressures upon us, all the thoughts that whir around inside our minds and spirits continue to be present in the stillness and space. They are like monkeys that loudly screech and shake the branches of our inner selves. In fact, they can be a greater challenge for us because in the stillness we are more consciously aware of them.

For many people it is the fear of what will happen when they stop that discourages them from rest. Largely this is because our response to hard times either mentally, spiritually or physically is to 'keep busy'. So we may find that when we take seriously the call to not only receive Sabbath but to live it, it takes us a while to adjust and become comfortable with the monkeys in our tree.

Islands in Time

There is a very real sense in which Sabbath is most commonly expressed as a set unit of time. For the Jewish communities through the ages, that has generally been from sunset on Friday evening to sunset on Saturday evening. There is a beautiful fluidity with the seasons here, as sunset in winter will be different from sunset in summer, and so there is an opportunity to mirror the patterns of rest we have already explored in God's creative world.

One of the most helpful definitions of Jewish Sabbath I have heard is as Sabbath as 'an island in time';[1] that this physical space is one which gives pause to the weary traveller on the seas of life providing a moment of refreshing. The day is punctuated by certain practices and customs, from lighting candles to begin and welcome Sabbath, sharing food together and parting blessings as the day closes. These have formed the centrepiece of Jewish life across the centuries. Jews also believe that on the Sabbath they receive a second soul for the day which enables them to focus on God and to feel Sabbath delight.

A question I still wrestle with is, how are we to live this day as Christians without feeling as though we have to enter into all the associated practices of Judaism?

Jesus was a Jew, as were his early disciples and the majority of the early church. They observed the practices and customs of the Jewish faith, and this included Sabbath. However, as the gospel spread outside of the Jewish community, and the Gentiles started coming to faith, this question came up time and time again. The answer was that non-Jewish believers were not bound to keep all of the laws of the Jewish faith, as what mattered most was following Jesus in whom the law had been fulfilled. As Paul says to the church in Colossae:

'Therefore do not let anyone condemn you in matters of food and drink or of observing festivals, new moons, or sabbaths. These are only a shadow of what is to come, but the substance belongs to Christ.'[2]

The danger for us as Christians is to think that because we are no longer bound to the law, because we follow the one in whom it is ultimately fulfilled, that the law is no longer important, so has nothing to say to us. The concept of an island in time, in the rough and dangerous seas of our busy world, has as much to say to us today as it did to the community of faith gathered on the slopes of Mount Sinai all those millennia ago. Just because we are not bound to observe it does not mean there is no value in this holy pause, or from taking the heart of it and expressing it through the freedom we now have in Christ.

One of the questions I was asked at the prayer breakfast was regarding those who worked in industries with non-standard working weeks. The example was used of a worker on an oil rig, who worked seven days a week several weeks at a time, and would find it impossible to honour a day of Sabbath during that period. What could Sabbath look like for that person? I am sure that there are other professions that spring to our minds that fit the same category.

My answer then, as now, would be to seek to express the heart of Sabbath in the context you find yourself in. For the oil worker it might be to take the non-working period of the day and to apply the heart of rest to that time. This is a principle that we were encouraged to take during our training at Spurgeon's College. The day is split into three periods: morning, afternoon and evening, and the general principle was that you only worked two of those three periods in any given day. This way you are honouring a pattern and rhythm of living that is not solely about work, but one that includes rest and gives the priority to life. This might not match the period of time of the Jewish Sabbath, but it does express the heart of it, especially for those who for valid reasons cannot keep a full day.

I believe that it is in this spirit that the prophet Isaiah encourages us to 'draw water from the wells of salvation'.[3] I have often felt encouraged on my own journey of faith by these words, and the use of the plural 'wells' by the prophet. God has not only provided us with one place of refreshing, one place and time of rest, but has blessed us with the ability to draw joyfully from different sources where he reveals them. Sabbath is an island in time, but perhaps on the voyage of life we need to do a bit of island hopping from time to time as the grace of God allows, discovering the different ways that rest can be found. One person's tropical paradise is another's marooned prison, so we need to be aware of what it is that gives us life, and to seek to live within this moment, or on this island. God longs for us to experience his life, to be infused with it, and that reality lies at the heart of living Sabbath.

Sabbath as Worship

The period of the Sabbath is not primarily focused on worship, at least in a traditional sense. Perhaps that understanding of the word is symptomatic of the struggles we have been exploring, that our worship too has been diluted to simply something that we 'do' at certain times, rather than an offering of our very selves to God. Paul gives the early church in Rome a wonderful definition of worship:

I appeal to you therefore, brothers and sisters, by the mercies of God, to present your bodies as a living sacrifice, holy and acceptable to God, which is your spiritual worship. Do not be conformed to this world, but be transformed by the renewing of your minds, so that you may discern what is the will of God – what is good and acceptable and perfect.[4]

There are two important parts of this appeal. Firstly, that the offering of our bodies sacrificially is an act of worship. Secondly, that doing so is part of the way that we are in tune with the will of God rather than the patterns of this world. As *The Message* puts it: 'Don't become so well-adjusted to your culture that you fit into it without even thinking.' Isn't that what most of us do when it comes to rest? Rather than offer our bodies, our lives, before God as an offering and act of worship, we simply allow ourselves to fit into the culture of the world around us. The worst part is that we so often do this without even thinking!

Sabbath rest is a time to offer ourselves to God, but it is also a time, as we saw earlier with the story of the city and country-dweller, to retune our ears to him.

Part of the worship of Sabbath was a remembering of what God had done for his people. In both the commandment passages of Exodus 20 and Deuteronomy 5, God's freeing his people from the slavery of Egypt is integral. These commands, and the way in which his people are to live, come as a result of, and are rooted in, who God is and what he has done. It is a call to remember transformed identity; to the world you may be defined by any number of things, but on this day you are reminded that you are defined by what God has done for you and who you are through him. It is a call to be set free from the things that hold you captive and to enter into the promises of

God. This Sabbath rest roots our identity in God. It is an active remembering of our God-given calling and identity in a world that is desperate to shape us in its own image. It is creating the space to remember, and to honour our Maker, the one who continues to make us in *his* image. Whole.

Our worship can face problems when it becomes about ritual rather than a living expression of relationship.

Several years ago Bex and I went on a tour of the Holy Land. When we visited Jerusalem, we stayed in a hotel that was just a short walk from the old city, which gave us the opportunity to be at the heart of one of the most significant and complex places on the planet.

Whilst at the hotel we noticed that there was a specially designated 'Sabbath elevator'. What made this elevator different from most was that there was no requirement to press any buttons, the lift would stop on every floor on the way up, and every floor on the way down. This meant that those wishing to observe the Sabbath requirements were not forced to break them through wanting to get to their hotel room.

The thirty-nine prohibited categories of work on the Sabbath contain within them some 1,500 individual rules. It is easy to receive the gift of Sabbath, but then become so bogged down trying to live it that you lose sight of the one you were meant to be drawing close to.

This is as much a challenge for us as Christians as it has been for the Jewish community. I remember speaking to a member of staff at a theological college about the subject matter for this book, about how it was hoping to be focused on the infusing of life that God longs for us to receive through his gift of rest, and the first question that I was asked was: 'Do you go shopping on a Sunday?' For so many Christians that it what Sabbath worship is: don't do your shopping on a Sunday! You can take part in the endless requirements of church life and of Sunday services to the point of exhaustion, so long as you stay clear of Sainsbury's.

Is that what it means to live Sabbath and keep it holy? Do we swap one set of requirements for another and miss the life that God is longing to bring us?

Perhaps there has been an assumption that Sabbath worship means that Sunday is the best day for it to take place. This was not the case for the early church, where there is little evidence that their non-Sabbath gatherings had replaced Sabbath.

For me Sunday is a work day and anything but a day of rest. It is not my island in time, it is a day when I feel a sense of work most acutely and feel more tired than most other days. It is not a day of receiving but of giving out. This is not just true for pastors, but for many who serve in lots of different ways to enable Sunday worship to happen. Even for those who attend services they can be anything but restful, whether it is the family trying to get everyone out of the door to avoid the glances of those who came 'on time'; or the disabled person who has to catch a bus, on a reduced timetable, to get to the service; rest is not often a word associated with Sunday mornings for Christians.

The history of why Sunday came to be seen as 'the Christian Sabbath' is a long and complex one which I do not propose to go into here. What has become clear as we progress further into the twenty-first century is that for some time now this concept has been increasingly adopted.

I have been in and around churches for most of my life, and they have been places where I have grown in my faith, been moved in worship, and encountered God in a life-changing way. However, they have also been places of pain, exhaustion and where the lens through which I see God has become fogged. Surely what God intended through the gift of Sabbath, and the command to not only receive it but to live it, was deeper than 10:30–11:45 a.m. once a week? As Marva Dawn honestly reflects: 'What a sad commentary it is on North American spirituality that the delight of "keeping the Sabbath day" has degenerated into the routine of drudgery – even the downright oppressiveness – of "going to church."'[5]

The same can be said for Christian spirituality in the United Kingdom as well.

So often our churches are places where the heart of Sabbath is smothered with church culture, rather than a means and a place to receive again the life of God, to be free to live that life, and to be rooted into the story of who God is and what he has done. There are certainly churches where this happens, and I have been blessed to be part of some that have, but they are rarer than we would care to honestly admit. Very often they can be places of 'anti-sabbath expectations and dispositions – entertainment, anonymity, consumption, appearance and self-exhibition'[6] that we see too often in the world around us.

What I increasingly believe lies at the heart of Sabbath is the concept of 'Soul Union'. Sabbath is sometimes portrayed as a bride to be welcomed, and the language of keeping the Sabbath clothed in the language of marriage. This is a sacred and holy union between God and his creation of which we are a part. Our living it in this way keeps it holy for us and honours it. It creates a space in which we enter into the very life of God himself, and through which our lives can be enriched and made whole. And surely this is worship! Worship is not confined to one day or indeed one place, but there is an intention about Sabbath rest, a seeking to lay down our 'everyday, ordinary life – our sleeping, eating, going-to-work, and walking-around life'[7] placing it before God as a worshipful offering, and to receive his life in its place.

Wherever this physical space and time is for you, Sunday, Saturday, or any other day of the week, let your heart be opened and your soul directed towards the one who gives you life. Honour that time, guard it and keep it as precious, as sacred, as intimate. It is far more than simply not doing, but it is about truly being – a time and space where, whatever the demands and pressure of the rest of the week are, you can honestly say: 'I am my beloved's and my beloved is mine . . .'[8]

Sabbath and Relationship

If Sabbath is a day when we are to choose life, then it is most certainly a day of relationship.

As we have already seen, God is a God of relationship, existing in perfect loving harmony as Father, Son and Holy Spirit. God is also the God who draws all of creation to himself, and calls us to care for and love one another as he has loved us.[9]

Sabbath is an expression of that relational foundation to the cosmos, with Dan Allender describing it as a 'dance with God and others'[10] where we can 'taste and see that the LORD is good'.[11]

Sabbath is not a day to be spent in isolation, adrift from the beauty and pleasure of the world, but a day to embrace the life that God has given, in him, in creation and in each other. 'There is no notion more at odds with the Sabbath than a day of forced quiet, spiritual exercises and religious devotion and attendance.'[12]

One of the things that has struck me as I have explored more about the meaning of Sabbath and what it means to live it, is that it is far deeper and wider-reaching than I had first imagined. What I used to believe was that this was a day when

you weren't allowed to do anything. It was a day of restriction
that as Christians we were blessed to be free from. What I increasingly feel is that it is a day when we are given the glorious
opportunity to rediscover and re-embrace God's full and free
life. That we are bound again in love to God, to creation and
to each other in a beautiful and profound way, if we make the
commitment not only to receive the gift but to live it.

So often in our mainstream Christian faith we have misun-
derstood the 'personal' and replaced it with 'ego'. Whilst I may
live out my faith in a community context, it is often lived in
tandem with others rather than in relationship with them.

Sabbath is a day when ego is laid aside, because there is
nothing that makes you understand your connections with
the world around you more than entering into it and seeing
it in all its glorious beauty. How can I look on the beauty of
the world God has made, the stars, the sunset, the vastness
of the sea, the variety of his creatures, and believe that the
world is really about me? Sabbath is a time to rediscover our
place in the world, to reconnect and to bask in the warmth of
relationship.

The world around us tells us often enough to look after ourselves, and we do not have to look very far to see that ultimately
the thing that suffers when we focus on ourselves to this degree
is relationship. In his book on the Ten Commandments, *Ten*,
J.John reflects on the Sabbath commandment: 'The most important things in life aren't things, but people.'[13]

Sabbath enables us to prioritize people over things and relationships over work. It allows us to give our families not the
sloppy seconds of our day, but the heart of it. It allows us to
invest in friendships old and new. It allows us to redirect our
focus and attention to the people that God has blessed us with
in our lives, to be a blessing to them and in turn be blessed.

It allows us to 'accentuate and nurture the gifts of God given to us and strengthen the memberships that make us whole'.[14]

Sabbath is far more wide-reaching than a space for reconnecting relationship; it is given as a means through which relationship can be restored. In Isaiah 56 we see the extension of the covenant following on from the list of excluded people in Deuteronomy who were not able to enter into the community. Here we see the space of welcome being extended:

> And the foreigners who join themselves to the LORD,
> to minister to him, to love the name of the LORD,
> and to be his servants,
> all who keep the sabbath, and do not profane it,
> and hold fast my covenant –
> these I will bring to my holy mountain,
> and make them joyful in my house of prayer;
> their burnt offerings and their sacrifices
> will be accepted on my altar;
> for my house shall be called a house of prayer
> for all peoples.[15]

What is incredible as you look at this passage, is not only the joyous fact that those who were once on the outside are now being brought into covenant relationship with the people of God, but the means through which they come: 'all who keep the sabbath'. Brueggemann reflects:

'How astonishing that of all the conditions for entry into the community the party of inclusiveness might have selected, they opted for Sabbath! They made Sabbath the single specific requirement for membership.'[16]

When we live Sabbath we create the space to restore that which is broken and to protect that which is vulnerable.

Reflecting on the Sabbath commandment J.John says: 'God's rest should be used to extend our relationships with family and friends.'[17]

One of the real benefits of the Jewish Sabbath is that the time is set and honoured by all. You do not have husbands celebrating Sabbath on a different day to their wives, or children from their parents, or friends from each other. Sabbath is a shared joy to be enjoyed by all. The challenge for those of us outside of this Jewish system is to seek to honour that principle in the way we structure our week. It is worth investing the time and effort to make this work well in the initial stages so that we can enjoy the benefits long-term, but like so many things, this does not just happen. We have to choose to accept the gift, and then in order to live it we have to choose to make it a priority. In Deuteronomy 30 the people of God are given the choice between life and death, blessings and curses. They are encouraged by God: 'Now choose life . . .'[18]

Sabbath is the place where we choose life in a culture that is increasingly bringing death to us as individuals and as families.

One of the most helpful phrases I have heard in ministry I read in a book by Peter Brain on sustainable ministry, where he uses the phrase 'our no's give value to our yes's'.[19] The concept is that you can only prioritize the things you want to say yes to if you learn to say no to other things. If relationships are to be a priority in our lives then we need to actively make them a priority by saying no to some of the other distractions of life that come our way. 'The first step to becoming a Sabbath home will therefore require that we learn to say no to the many pressures to do or accomplish more.'[20]

What Sabbath rest also offers us is the ability to live out a new identity. So often we allow ourselves to be defined by what we do, which seems fine as long as we are doing that well.

However when we cease to 'do it well', or things get hard, then it is easy for us to draw the conclusion that the problem must be me. Rarely is that the case. We live with tremendous pressure today, with the media and social media in particular calling us to measure up to impossible standards of success, health, wealth and happiness. Even social media platforms that offer the ability to be better connected with others, actually separates us from them because we end up comparing our lives to theirs. When we do that, we rarely measure up.

The world we live in barely gives us a moment to breathe, to reflect, to simply be; to look inside and to reconnect with who God has created us to be. Sabbath is a time to be, a time to breathe and to match our internal breathing to the rhythm of creation. It is a time to listen, not to the many voices around us, but to the still small voice of truth whose whispers resonate deep within our DNA. We long for that resonance, those imaginal cells that offer us a vision of a different reality, a different way of living that is not defined by activity alone, but by the hope that transformation can occur. Transformation in the way we see ourselves, in our relationships with others and in our worship. If Sabbath rest is indeed an island in time, then it is an island that can bring transformation to time itself.

Whilst Sabbath can appear to be eclipsed by other New Testament subject matter, what we see is that it does break through the sheer volume of other teaching. This is reflective of the life we live. We do not live a 24/7 Sabbath, but rather Sabbath as a way of life breaks through the sheer volume of our lives as we know them.

If we can receive it, grasp it and not let go, fight for it and live it, really live it, then what takes flight from the chrysalis of our rest is far more beautiful than we could have ever imagined, and nothing can ever quite be the same again.

6

Lord of the Sabbath

Jesus was not so much redefining Sabbath, as many have suggested, but is redefining, or perhaps restoring, what it means to be holy.

Recently the nation was wowed by the wedding of Prince Harry and Meghan Markle. The crowds gathered expectantly days before the date itself wanting to get a good spot on the route, the bands and the soldiers had rehearsals in their colourful and shining uniforms. Even the weather seemed to have been booked in advance. As their day got closer many felt a sense of anticipation and excitement, and when it arrived it did not fail to deliver. There seemed to be a smooth effortlessness about the way that all they had planned and hoped for became reality.

Tom Wright says of the Sabbath that it was 'the moment during which one sensed the outward movement of history from its first foundations to its ultimate resolution'.[1]

Sabbath showed that God's people were moving somewhere, caught up within an eternal purpose that looked towards God's fulfilment.

The law was the forerunner, pointing and clearing the way for the one who would come later to fulfil it: Jesus. It seemed that not only God's people but the whole cosmos was gathering expectantly for this long-awaited moment in history, in their story. That all the bright and shining colour of the God of creation was to burst into our reality in a new way, carrying with it all the hopes of the world. When the moment arrived, it seemed anything but smooth and effortless.

The one who had come to fulfil the law clashed on a regular basis with those who saw it as their role to uphold it. For me, and probably many others growing up in the church, my understanding of the Sabbath came from either reciting the commands in Sunday school or hearing of the ongoing battle between Jesus and the Pharisees about breaking it. Neither provide a rich understanding of the nature of rest or the way Jesus saw it.

Before we look at a couple of examples from the gospels, I wanted to explore one element of Jesus' teaching which will I think inform our journey in this chapter.

> Then he [Jesus] said to them all, 'If any want to become my followers, let them deny themselves and take up their cross daily and follow me.'[2]

I had often understood this passage to be wholly about self-denial to the point even of laying down your life, but there is an element of this verse which we often overlook and so miss out on a deep heartbeat of Jesus' ministry. If Jesus had simply wanted to talk about laying down your life in the face of persecution, there were better metaphors to use than the cross. The religious leaders of the day had branded Jesus and his followers as dangerous blasphemers, and it was far more likely that they would be stoned to death. This was the fate of the first recorded martyr, Stephen, after all.[3] Stoning was the punishment for breaking the law; the cross was very different. The cross was the punishment for those who rebelled against the establishment. It was the punishment of revolutionaries. So what is Jesus calling his disciples to? What would they have understood that call to be in their day? Part of the denial of self Jesus is speaking about here is about living in the face of the prevailing powers of the day. All that was oppressive, unjust and de-relational, wherever it may be found, needed to be challenged through the powerful and redeeming scope of God's love in Christ. I have learned that it is never wise to try to give black and white statements about what was happening at the cross, but surely this has to be part of it.

That was the call to those first disciples, too, to lead a life that when it comes face to face with injustice, oppression, abuse and evil, stands in revolutionary contrast to them. This is, at least in part, what it means to take up your cross, and seen in this way we can view Jesus' teachings on Sabbath in a richer light. We can see that what is needed, in the face of a prevailing twenty-first-century culture which expresses a view of work that causes great pain and distress to many, is a revolutionary stand against such a system. Sabbath expresses within itself a heart of rest which is not only a tonic to the ills of our time, but is a form of active rebellion against a system which seeks to express the value of a person based primarily on what they do. Jean Vanier, founder of the L'Arche community,[4] speaks of the challenge of being too attached to our function, and experiencing burnout.[5] We will come to look more at that later. This self-sufficiency, believing we stand on our own achievements, not only stands in opposition to the cross of Christ, where we find and rest in our identity through the grace of God, but leads to our 'rejection of finding a harmonious rhythm of life'.[6]

Much of Christian debate these days seems to polarize people into one of two opposing camps. There is a danger when we come to look at Jesus and the Sabbath that we will simply read into these passages that which we already believe. That of course is the great danger when it comes to Scripture more widely. We view life through the lens of our experience, culture, social status and many other subtle facets that focus how we see the world. One of the biggest mistakes we can make is to fail to realize that this is what we are doing, to believe that this is the only way to see the world, or faith, or to think that this is what it must surely look like for everyone else. When we do this, we polarize that lens to block out the light that comes from unwanted sources because we cannot cope with the uncomfortable glare. However, as the apostle Paul can attest to from his eventful journey to Damascus, sometimes it is the unexpected light that has the greatest impact.

There are around fifty mentions of Sabbath in the gospels, and certainly not space to engage with them all here. There are, however, two key passages regarding Jesus and the Sabbath which I invite us to explore in the spirit of being open to see not simply what we expect or want to see, but the unexpected light of Christ coming in new ways.

Lord of the Sabbath

At that time Jesus went through the grainfields on the sabbath; his disciples were hungry, and they began to pluck heads of grain and to eat. When the Pharisees saw it, they said to him, 'Look, your disciples are doing what is not lawful to do on the sabbath.' He said to them, 'Have you not read what David did when he and his companions were hungry? He entered the house of God

and ate the bread of the Presence, which it was not lawful for
him or his companions to eat, but only for the priests. Or have
you not read in the law that on the sabbath the priests in the
temple break the sabbath and yet are guiltless? I tell you, something greater than the temple is here. But if you had known
what this means, "I desire mercy and not sacrifice," you would
not have condemned the guiltless. For the Son of Man is lord of
the sabbath.'[7]

Here we have an account of Jesus and his disciples walking
through a field in Galilee and plucking the heads of the corn
to stave off hunger. It's a wonderful scene that it doesn't take
much imagination to jump right into the heart of. Having
probably been at the synagogue, which was his custom, they
now walk together in their local fields. There is no indica-
tion that they have broken any of the other Sabbath laws
to this point, yet they are being shadowed by the Pharisees.
Often the world seems safer if we can separate it into goodies
and baddies. We have got into a knee-jerk habit of Pharisee-
bashing over the centuries, but despite their often being
viewed as the villains in the story, they were not in the habit
of hiding out in Galilean cornfields in order to catch the
average Sabbath-breaker in the act. But Jesus was not your
average person, and so the Pharisees would have taken the
opportunity to follow him, to observe him and to take advantage of any perceived slip-up. This explains their presence
in the field that day.

So in what way were the disciples breaking the commandment? One of the forbidden activities on the Sabbath was har-
vesting, which is exactly what the disciples were doing, and which
put them at the very least in conflict with the Torah tradition of
the Pharisees.[8]

Whether or not the actual Sabbath commandment was broken has been debated by commentators for many years with differing opinions. I do not wish to focus so much on that particular question, but to think a little bit more about how Jesus chooses to respond to the accusation that the Pharisees make.

There are three in particular I wish to highlight.

Firstly, there is the recalling of the story of David and his followers from 1 Samuel 21.

There are some commentators who have suggested that Jesus uses this story as a simple legal rebuff of the Pharisees' accusation. The bread in the account Jesus quotes was placed in the tabernacle for the Sabbath, and the point has been made that Jesus is essentially saying 'if it was reasonable for David then surely it is reasonable for others'[9]. However, by linking himself with David in this way, Jesus is making a far deeper point about who he is, and about what the Sabbath means.

David has already been anointed as God's chosen king in 1 Samuel 16, and is now on the run from the rejected King Saul. As Tom Wright says, 'Jesus is the true king; like David, he has been anointed, but not yet enthroned.'[10] In choosing David and rejecting Saul, God was not rejecting kingship, although kingship was never God's best, but the brokenness of the one through whom it was interpreted. In a similar way, in God's choosing and anointing of Christ, he was not rejecting the law, but the legalism of the Pharisees through whom it was interpreted, who placed traditional systems over the needs of human beings. He is not rejecting the Sabbath, but the systems that are placed around it which, paradoxically, actually keep people from experiencing its life.

Secondly, in the parallel to this passage in Mark chapter 2 we read: 'The sabbath was made for humankind, and not humankind for the sabbath . . .'[11]

Sabbath is made for humankind 'and without it we become less than human. God has made us to need both work and rest, and the boundaries between them'.[12]

As we have already explored in some depth, God has given the Sabbath as a gift not a burden, but the endless rules and regulations of the Pharisees had made it a burden to the people. It had become about religious observance and not about life and freedom. When we look back to the prophet Isaiah we read:

> If you refrain from trampling the sabbath,
> from pursuing your own interests on my holy day;
> if you call the sabbath a delight
> and the holy day of the LORD honorable;
> if you honor it, not going your own ways,
> serving your own interests, or pursuing your own affairs;
> then you shall take delight in the LORD,
> and I will make you ride upon the heights of the earth;
> I will feed you with the heritage of your ancestor Jacob,
> for the mouth of the LORD has spoken.[13]

The Sabbath was meant to be about delight and blessing, riding upon the heights of the earth. Where was the expression of this language in the Sabbath regulations of Jesus' day? Where is it in our expressions of Sabbath and rest today?

To understand this statement of Jesus a little better, let's think for a moment about the opening words of the fourth commandment: 'Remember the sabbath day, and keep it holy.'

So often I have heard the misquoting of this verse in its stopping short of the word 'holy'. We are not simply commanded to *keep* the Sabbath, through some sense of religious obligation. We are commanded to keep it *holy*. We have already explored what that might have meant for God's people, but it is into this arena that the verse from Mark 2:27 is placed.

Jesus was not so much redefining Sabbath, as many have suggested, but is redefining, or perhaps restoring, what it means to be holy.

So often we have defined holiness in regard to sin. If you eliminate that, then what remains must be holiness. Rather, as always, our beginning should be God. That is the essence of what God says to his people in Leviticus 20:26: 'You must be holy because I, the LORD, am holy. I have set you apart from all other people to be my very own' (NLT).

There is again that language of being set apart, but we also now see the reason: 'to be my very own'. There is a relational dynamic, a love dynamic right at the centre of holiness. God's holiness cannot be removed and separated from his love, and for Jesus everything is viewed and interpreted through the prism of God's love. As Irvin Zeitlin says in his book *Jesus and the Judaism of His Time*: 'For him [Jesus] the chief criterion for the validity of a specific *halakhah* (ordinance) is its compatibility with the love command.'[14] That love command is that which we see expressed so clearly by Jesus quoting from and expanding on the words of Deuteronomy and Leviticus:

'You shall love the Lord your God with all your heart, and with all your soul, and with all your mind.' This is the greatest and first commandment. And a second is like it: 'You shall love your neighbor as yourself.' On these two commandments hang all the law and the prophets.[15]

Relationship. Love of God, love of neighbour and love of self. All the law, including the Sabbath, hangs on this. Sabbath is not about rules and regulations, but about love of God, love of neighbour, and love of self. As James Dunn says: 'What was at stake in Jesus' controversies regarding the law was not matters of scholastic definition and dispute but the right relations between God and his people, and among his people.'[16]

What about our patterns of rest? Have they become a stale and obligation-fuelled ritual, or do they express love of God, love of neighbour and love of self?

Thirdly, the words of Jesus at the end of this passage: 'For the Son of Man is lord of the sabbath.'[17]

What does it mean for Jesus to be Lord of the Sabbath? To explore what it means for Jesus to be Lord would require far more time and space for exploration than we have here, but for the purpose of our discussion, could we express it like this? Jesus is the one through whom the redemptive and restorative love of God finds its fullest expression, not just for humanity, but for the whole cosmos. As Paul writes to the church in Colossae:

> He was supreme in the beginning and – leading the resurrection parade – he is supreme in the end. From beginning to end he's there, towering far above everything, everyone. So spacious is he, so roomy, that everything of God finds its proper place in him without crowding. Not only that, but all the broken and dislocated pieces of the universe – people and things, animals and atoms – get properly fixed and fit together in vibrant harmonies, all because of his death, his blood that poured down from the cross.[18]

We think of 'Lord' as a hierarchical term, but for Jesus what it meant to be Lord was also the power of redemptive love. It was a fresh start for the Sabbath, redefined once more, not through the rules and regulations of the religious, but through the holiness and self-giving love of God. As Bishop Curry said at the wedding of Prince Harry and Meghan Markle, quoting Dr Martin Luther King, we need to discover love's redemptive power, and when we do, we'll be able to make a new world of this old one.

When David was anointed as king it marked a new beginning, a beginning of the rule of the one who was 'after [God's] own heart'.[19] Now we see in the Lordship of Jesus a new beginning, a new rule of the one who is in 'the very heart of the Father'.[20]

So the Sabbath as seen through Jesus is not simply about a lack of activity in and of itself, but it is a laying down of that which is ours in order to take up that which is God's. It is a laying down of our lives in order to be infused with his. It is rooting ourselves within his love, and in that rooting it is to discover the seeds of transformation, to be made new and to help to shape a new world. It is a longing deep within our spirits for the delights of Paul's prayer for the Ephesians to be a reality for us:

> I pray that you may have the power to comprehend, with all the saints, what is the breadth and length and height and depth, and to know the love of Christ that surpasses knowledge, so that you may be filled with all the fullness of God.[21]

How Much More Valuable

> He left that place and entered their synagogue; a man was there with a withered hand, and they asked him, 'Is it lawful to cure on the sabbath?' so that they might accuse him. He said to them, 'Suppose one of you has only one sheep and it falls into a pit on the sabbath; will you not lay hold of it and lift it out? How much more valuable is a human being than a sheep! So it is lawful to do

good on the sabbath.' Then he said to the man, 'Stretch out your hand.' He stretched it out, and it was restored, as sound as the other. But the Pharisees went out and conspired against him, how to destroy him.[22]

One of the hotly debated questions in the passages where Jesus heals on the Sabbath is, does Jesus actually break the Sabbath commandment? There are varying opinions on this, and certainly there are occasions where he violates the Pharisees' laws regarding the Sabbath. I recently heard a discussion that offered a passionate defence of Jesus' actions when posed the question as to whether Jesus had broken the Sabbath commandment. The basic line of argument was that if Jesus 'violated' the law of God by breaking the Sabbath commandment, then he sinned. Because we affirm that Jesus was without sin, he could not have broken the Sabbath commandment. Simple . . .

But to view it in this way is like peeling an apple, eating only the peel and throwing away the rest of the apple. The apple is the substance of the story, and at the centre of the substance is the core of the message. At the centre of the core are seeds; seeds of transformation. The question for the Pharisees is: 'Did Jesus break the Sabbath commandment?' The question for Jesus is: 'What is Sabbath?' As Lord of the Sabbath, it is Jesus who gets to define it.

Notice that in both the passages we are exploring here Jesus does not reject the Sabbath, or view it as unimportant. To take this view from the gospel accounts of Jesus and the Sabbath would be a profound misreading of them. 'Jesus did not reject the Jewish law. He sometimes disagreed with its interpretation or application by some of his contemporaries, but they also disagreed among themselves.'[23] A prime example of this is the one Jesus uses in this encounter about the sheep falling into a pit on the Sabbath. This question about the sheep might seem like a rural anecdote, but it actually comes from a very real debate happening amongst religious teachers of the day. The debate centred on how much you were willing to give up for God in your pursuit of holiness, specifically using this example as a means of illustrating that question in the context of Sabbath. There were of course those who said that it was perfectly reasonable to rescue an animal sucked into a pit on the Sabbath, because to do so was to save life. This was allowed on the Sabbath, and when in doubt, the benefit was given to the act of saving life rather than the strict regulation. So if a sheep did fall down a pit, and there was any doubt about whether its life was in danger, then it was perfectly acceptable for those who held this interpretation to rescue it on the Sabbath.

There were also those who took a much stricter view. In the Qumran community, known for its piety and rigorous observance of the law, they held the opinion that if the animal fell into a pit on the Sabbath, then you were not allowed to rescue it. More than that, they held that if a person fell into a pit on the Sabbath, then they should not be rescued in a way that broke the Sabbath regulations.[24]

On this matter, Jesus and the Pharisees would have probably agreed on a different interpretation to the Qumran community, one which valued the life of the animal as more important than the Sabbath regulation. That is at the heart of Jesus' challenge to them. 'Suppose one of you has only one sheep and it falls into a pit on the sabbath; will you not lay hold of it and lift it out?' Of course you would, because you know the value and worth of the animal and you want to make sure that it doesn't come to harm. 'How much more valuable is a human being than a sheep!' If you are willing to allow the Sabbath regulations to be interpreted to bless and care for this animal, how can that not be the case for this man, who is more valuable to God than the sheep? What is the criteria that Jesus uses, then, for activity on the Sabbath? Doing good? That's the way it seems from how he ends his conversation with the Pharisees, 'it is lawful to do good on the sabbath.'

But remember that the thrust of Jesus' argument is also relational, it is about this man. If the Sabbath can benefit the sheep but not the person in need, then where is the life in the Sabbath?

As we have seen, Sabbath is a means through which we are infused with God's life, it is a means through which we experience that life in real and tangible ways. It is not simply about saving life, but experiencing it. Jesus asks the man to stretch out his hand and he is healed.

In this stage of our journey together we have seen how Jesus has come to root Sabbath in who God is, the one who brings new life, life in all its fullness. The regulations that get in the way of that, that end up stopping people from experiencing life, are what Jesus implies are anti-Sabbath.

So as we reflect on our own lives, what are the patterns of rest that bring us life? What are the patterns that get in the way of that life, perhaps because we are doing them out of a sense of duty? Do your patterns of rest bring you delight? Do they cause you to soar upon the heights? Do you look forward to them, or have they become a burden or simply about recovery?

When we look at Jesus and the Sabbath, we see the freedom to express who we are in relationship with God and one another. We see love of God, love of neighbour and love of self, and find those loves settling into their proper place in our lives and our life together. 'When he declared himself to be Lord of the Sabbath he was presenting himself as the guardian and interpreter of the Sabbath, not the abolisher of it.'[25]

Tony Horsfall's book *Working from a Place of Rest* explores key aspects of this theme in the life of Jesus. He, like many others, explores the challenges of keeping Sabbath today, but also that strong sense of it as a gift we see graciously redefined in Jesus. It is through Jesus we find our ultimate rest, our eternal Sabbath, the one who comes to infuse us with the life of God. His claim, that he has come that we might have life and 'have it abundantly'[26] is the great Sabbath invitation where wholeness can not only be found, but experienced in a greater measure than we have ever previously known.

Is Sabbath for the Christian? Perhaps that question has different layers, but I would simply say this: if Jesus is Lord of the Sabbath, the one in whom we find the very life of God; if Jesus himself kept and honoured Sabbath; if he taught his disciples the full meaning of Sabbath; then it is certainly not something as Christians we should shy away from exploring.

7

Come to Me

Come to me, all you that are weary and are carrying heavy burdens, and I will give you rest.

Jesus[1]

I have always loved John's gospel. There is a quote that my mum first introduced me to, although who it originates from has been the subject of much debate over the years, describing the waters of John's gospel as 'shallow enough for a child to paddle in but deep enough for an elephant to swim in'.[2] In John's gospel we are given many of the richest passages in all of Scripture, including what we often refer to as the 'I am' sayings of Jesus.

In John 8:12 we read that Jesus said, 'I am the light of the world.' He came to bring light to those living in deep darkness, to bring colour and warmth and heat and sustenance and all that light is associated with.

Through the light of the Son of God, who has entered our humanity, we can now see more clearly. We can see who God truly and eternally is, we can see hope, blessing and transformation in our lives each and every day. When you read the gospel and see the transformation of the lives of those he came into contact with, then there is little else that makes sense than to agree with the words he said, Jesus is the light of the world. The speed of light is approximately 186,000 miles per second, which is mind-boggling. It means that the light leaving our sun will reach us around eight minutes and twenty seconds later, travelling 93,000,000 miles in that time. In recent scientific tradition, the speed of light has been constant wherever you are in the cosmos. With the exception of around two thousand years ago where in a small forgotten province of a Roman occupied territory it seems that light was moving at around three miles per hour. This light that came to bring life to everyone didn't burst forth as a solar flare, but walked through the dust and the dirt of our humanity, shining life, person by person. He could have announced it any way, seared into the skies like an aurora, but he chose to do it on foot. It seems that God was not in a rush.

Whilst we have seen the transformative teachings of Jesus when it comes to the Sabbath, redefining what it means to be holy, we now get to slow the pace, and simply walk with Jesus into the encounters of rest we see throughout the gospels.

Few Things Are Necessary

Now as they went on their way, he entered a certain village, where a woman named Martha welcomed him into her home. She had a sister named Mary, who sat at the Lord's feet and listened to what he was saying. But Martha was distracted by her many tasks; so she came to him and asked, 'Lord, do you not care that my sister has left me to do all the work by myself? Tell her then to help me.' But the Lord answered her, 'Martha, Martha, you are worried and distracted by many things; there is need of only one thing. Mary has chosen the better part, which will not be taken away from her.'[3]

You may be familiar with the story from Luke's gospel. You may well have been asked, or asked yourself, whether you are a Mary or a Martha. Someone else might have put being a Mary or a Martha onto you. Perhaps it is time to look again at this passage to see how it can speak to us on our journey.

Mary and Martha live in a little town called Bethany, which is to the east of Jerusalem on the slopes of the Mount of Olives. It was a place where Jesus stayed often when he was in the area. Mary, Martha and Lazarus were close to Jesus, and their home provided much-needed friendship, safety and rest for him.

It is important to say that both Mary and Martha loved Jesus, but we can often get the impression that Mary was more devoted to Jesus than the busy Martha. I think to take that away from this text would not only read into it something that is not there, but fly in the face of what we see in the rest of the gospels.

For a moment I want to focus on Martha, because whether we would choose to associate ourselves with her or not, this is a moment most of us can relate to. Luke tells us that Martha is 'distracted by her many tasks', presumably the tasks of hospitality for Jesus,[4] and later, Jesus gently challenges her, saying, 'Martha, Martha, you are worried and distracted by many things . . .' Distraction and anxiety are a very real and present part of life. There are so many things that need to be done, so many tasks to be accomplished, so many people that we need to keep happy, that life at times can feel like spinning plates, and God forbid that any should drop.

The anxiety of doing too much distracts us, and part of the problem for Martha here in our passage is what she is being distracted from. She is so busy working to serve Jesus that she forgets to sit and rest with him. That is something I can very much relate to. How much of my Christian service has been devoted to 'doing things for God' rather than simply being with him! This is not so much a physical time and space issue now, as perhaps it might have been in Sabbath, but an attitude of heart. Martha was doing a good thing, the thing that was expected when showing hospitality. And she is, and perhaps we would be too, really upset that she is the one lumped with all the work and Mary is sitting around doing nothing. It's as though Martha says: 'There should be no time to rest when there is work to be done! Don't you care, Jesus, that I am the one left to do all the work?'

I have had to learn to be protective over my time off, because I know that if I am not, other than Bex, no one else will be. Have you learned to guard your time? Are there others who can help you to practically set aside the time you need to rest and be infused with the life of God? Is your life punctuated by God's life or punctured by the distractions of the many things you are desperately whizzing around trying to do?

I think the distraction is to become so busy with doing what is expected that we end up having no time and space to rest at all, no time and space to be infused with the life of God because we are so focused on serving him. Serving him is a wonderful thing, don't get me wrong, wherever you are and in whatever way you have been called to. It's something that should be our delight as well as our duty, but one of the difficult but releasing things I have learned over recent years, is that God does not need me. The fate of the kingdom does not rest with me. The salvation of the world does not rest with me. The work of the church does not rest with me. God does not *need* me. When I can embrace

that, then I am free to sit at his feet and embrace the stillness amid the tasks. This acknowledgement does not make the
tasks go away, but it simply states that I am not so bound to
them that I am distracted from what God's best for me is at
that time.

The danger is with this passage, that we assume it means
that all work is bad and all rest is good. That rest is better than
work. I don't think that is what Jesus or Luke is saying here. As
William Barclay says: 'There is no right or wrong in this. God
did not make everyone alike.'[5]

There may be some of us who find it easier to work than
rest, and there may be others who find rest easier. That is not
the point. It wasn't that Martha's work was wrong, but that it
was done at the wrong time. This was the time when she was
meant to be resting with Jesus, ready to receive from and be
with him, keeping company with her guest. In his commentary on Luke, Darrell Bock reminds us: 'Often in the hustle
and bustle of life, we need to pause for a moment of reflection
before the Lord.'[6]

Whilst this worshipful reflectiveness may not be what
springs to mind when we think of rest, what it does show us
is the value of stopping for that which is greater. It shows us
the value of stopping in order to rediscover who we are in the
presence of the one who is the light of life. It reminds us that
there is something other than what we feel is needed; indeed, as
the early manuscripts of this passage put it, Jesus answers 'few
things are necessary'. How much of our work – of what occu-
pies our thoughts and time, that drives us to rush and to worry,
that causes us to be distracted – is necessary? It is a question we
might too quickly rush to answer before we think again of the
context. How much of it is necessary when the alternative is to
be still at the feet of Jesus?

Here is my simple definition of what it means: 'Stopping is pausing for a few minutes, or a few hours, or a few days, to remember
who I am and why I am here.'[7]

As a follower of Jesus, who I am can never fully be defined
simply by what I do, but by what has been done by the one at
whose feet Mary sits. In a world where work continues to seek
to define who we are rather than simply what we do, what else
can be more necessary?

Come to the Well

[H]e left Judea and started back to Galilee. But he had to go
through Samaria. So he came to a Samaritan city called Sychar,
near the plot of ground that Jacob had given to his son Joseph. Jacob's well was there, and Jesus, tired out by his journey, was sitting
by the well. It was about noon.[8]

Another encounter where we discover rest is in John chapter 4.
John tells us that Jesus is travelling from Judea to Galilee, a
distance of some seventy miles. Depending on how often they
stopped and any demands on Jesus' time along the route, this
journey would have taken between four days and a week to
make on foot. This was not easy ground to cover, and Jesus
and the disciples were not using walking boots picked up from
the nearest outdoor pursuits store. It was a long, tiring and
hot walk.

Now there may well have been a reason for Jesus not to stop
in this particular area. It wasn't that Samaritans and Jews simply
did not get along, there was a deep ethnic hatred between them.
Perhaps we might go as far as to compare it to the relationship

between Israel and Palestine today; two people groups sharing the same space but seemingly irreconcilably different. Jesus and the disciples may have been justified in hurrying through this space to the friendlier territory to the north.

What about the important work in Galilee? Surely there can be no time to stop and rest whilst there are souls to be won for the kingdom? For Jesus, Galilee could wait, and he could stop and rest. This God of the three-mile-per-hour light was not in a rush; there were things to do in Sychar, and the first was to rest. 'He was aware of his own tiredness and he knew the remedy.'[9]

On our journey of life there are many demands on our time, as we have seen with Martha. Sometimes our work can be a joy; it can feel light, cool and refreshing. But at other times it is a long, tiring and hot walk that takes us into uncomfortable territory. What that territory looks like for each of us will be different; the landscape will be uniquely shaped. The territory of burnout, or stress, or depression, or exhaustion, or relational breakdown; these are all areas that we can sometimes find ourselves in when the walk of life is unrelentingly hard and long. What do we do in those times? Well, this passage gives us a wonderful double blessing to give us hope.

Firstly, Jesus stopped. Just let those words sink in for a moment. Jesus – stopped. Jesus was not so much driven as responsive. He was not driven by the demands of others, or the social conventions of his time, or the religious and ethnic fractures of this region. He was responsive, in this moment, to his own needs. He knew he needed to rest, and if Jesus can rest, so can we. This short verse in John 4:6 gives us permission to take care of ourselves by stopping to rest. In this uncomfortable territory, Jesus stops to rest. I don't mean to labour the point but it seems countercultural not just to the ministry, but other professions and to the work ethic of our day that tells us to battle through. To battle through tiredness, to battle through anxiety, to battle through depression and stress and exhaustion, to battle through relational breakdown; keep going, it will get better. I have rarely seen that end happily. I know from my own experience that if we do not learn from Jesus here at the well, and stop to rest, eventually circumstances will force us to do just that, because we cannot carry on any further, and often the cost is high. Rest is not simply therapeutic. It is not the remedy for our battered bodies and souls, it is partly the means through which we can avoid our bodies and souls becoming battered in the first place.

Secondly, because Jesus stops to rest he encounters the woman at the well, and as a result of that encounter, her life and the lives of many in that village were changed for ever. Rest is not just of benefit to us, but it is of benefit and a blessing to those around us. Being responsive to ourselves in learning self-care, in learning to stop and rest, means that we have the space to be responsive to others too.

All by Yourselves

The apostles gathered around Jesus, and told him all that they had done and taught. He said to them, "Come away to a deserted place all by yourselves and rest a while." For many were coming and going, and they had no leisure even to eat. And they went away in the boat to a deserted place by themselves.[10]

There is a lot going on in Mark 6. It is the longest chapter in Mark's gospel, and is in the top ten longest chapters out of eighty-nine in all four gospels. In Mark 6:7–13 he sends the disciples out to the villages in Galilee to proclaim the good news of the kingdom. We do not know how long the disciples are away for, but we do know from verses 12 and 13 that it was a fairly full ministry time: 'So they went out and proclaimed that all should repent. They cast out many demons, and anointed with oil many who were sick and cured them.'[11]

This is emphasized in the passage we began this section with, where Mark notes, having returned from this time in the villages, that they had not even had time to eat anything.

Whilst rest is not always about 'getting away from it all', there are times when life has been so busy that we do need to come away all by ourselves to rest a while.

There are almost a dozen times in the gospels when Jesus chooses to 'get away' to either rest or pray, either on his own or with the disciples. The demands on Jesus' time are not exaggerated in the gospels; people flocked to see him. Even this small retreat with Jesus and the disciples so they could have some food ends with them sharing that lunch with thousands of others. But in the middle of the business of ministry and life, Jesus knows how valuable it is to reclaim time in order to be refreshed and infused with life.

This idea of reclaiming or even redeeming time is an interesting one which is worth reflecting on here for a moment.

The thrust of Paul's argument in Ephesians 5 is that we are to imitate the life of God shown through the giving of his Son in love. Essentially we are to be infused with the life of God through the sacrificial offering of Jesus. Paul goes on to say:

'Sleeper, awake!
Rise from the dead,
and Christ will shine on you.'
Be careful then how you live, not as unwise people but as wise, making the most of the time, because the days are evil.[12]

The phrase in particular that stands out for our discussion is 'making the most of the time'. Now there would be some who would interpret this as 'don't waste any opportunity' or 'make sure that you are doing all you can to be productive for God'. That's the way we often see time, as a commodity, the use of which we have to justify, if not to others, then to ourselves and ultimately to God. We have to make the most of it, don't waste it. However, when we look at the word we translate to 'make the most of', then we get a different picture. The word ἐξαγοραζό basically means 'to buy back from the marketplace'. Tony Horsfall reflects that 'what Paul is saying here is not "Try to get more done in even less time", but exactly the opposite. He is saying, "Don't let your idea of time be conditioned by the marketplace, but rescue it and use it in God's way".'[13]

So every time Jesus takes those restful moments to get away; every time the disciples do the same; every time you and I seek to imitate Jesus in this way, we are redeeming time from the marketplace. We are saying that there is another use for that time than simply commercial. We are living in rebellion to the culture that presses demand after demand on us, like walking through a busy marketplace with sellers shouting out to get our attention.

I recently heard a programme on BBC Radio 2[14] where the host was interviewing the leader of a political party advocating a four-day working week. The thrust of the argument in favour of this was to 'get back time' for ourselves, rather than having to try to cram too much into life. The host introduced the programme by referring to the Japanese word '*Karōshi*', which can literally be translated as 'overwork death'. It seems, then, that the need to buy back time has a very real urgency in a global marketplace culture where some are literally working themselves to death.

What are the areas of your life where you need to buy back time from the marketplace? To redeem time?

When Mary sits at the feet of Jesus, she is buying back time from the marketplace. When Jesus sits on the well in Sychar, he is buying back time from the marketplace. When the disciples get into the boat for a bite to eat, they are buying back time from the marketplace. This process of rest is not simply restorative but it is redemptive, it brings our humanity into alignment with the fullness of God and humanity found in Christ, the one who in the business of our frenetic lives calls us to 'come away'.

I Will Give You Rest . . .

> Are you tired? Worn out? Burned out on religion? Come to me. Get away with me and you'll recover your life. I'll show you how to take a real rest. Walk with me and work with me – watch how I do it. Learn the unforced rhythms of grace. I won't lay anything heavy or ill-fitting on you. Keep company with me and you'll learn to live freely and lightly.[15]

The above quote is taken from *The Message*, which beautifully and poetically conveys these words of Jesus in Matthew's gospel. It is one of the most well-known invitations of Jesus, and probably the one that springs to mind when we think of rest. Tom Wright describes it as 'the most welcoming and encouraging invitation ever offered'.[16]

Let's take time to move through these words of invitation for a moment and see what God might be saying to us on our journey.

Are you tired? Worn out? Burned out on religion?

How many times in my life would I have raised my hand to most of these questions? In my heart it would be many, but I sense that if I had actually been asked them directly, I would have been slightly more evasive with my answers. I think that is probably because I didn't know at the time how tired, worn out and burned out I was. I had grown up with faith, tried to follow Jesus in the everyday moments of life, through school, college and work. When I trained for ministry it was a wonderful time, but it was life in a bubble. A very helpful bubble to learn and to grow, to have the freedom to be shaped by God and trained by wonderful women and men. When the bubble burst as we entered our first pastorate, it burst hard. The issues we faced were not the issues we had discussed and journeyed with in our lecture rooms. The demands of change management overwhelmed the pastoral ones. I remember reading a meme once that said 'if you want people to like you don't be a pastor, sell ice cream'. There is certainly truth in that. It is a hard truth to live out when it feels like the members of your congregation are coming to you all demanding different flavours, with some insisting that theirs should be the only flavour you sell. For this world, this church, I felt very unprepared.

After a while this mindset tired me out, wore me down and I began to replace a genuinely hopeful faith with a theological form of ice-cream selling. I worked more and more hours trying to keep up with the demands I was coping less and less with, withdrawing from people around me. It was only an unexpected moment of breakthrough which brought me back into reality and helped me to see just how worn down I was.

Your answers to these questions may be different, and how your tiredness manifested itself may also be different. Each of us, though, must face the truth that we can be prone to these realities. It does us no good to keep on keeping on, or ignore the honest answers to these questions, because if we do then we and those we love will end up suffering as a result. It is only when we acknowledge the reality of our situation that we are open to the grace of God that can in time bring healing and a greater wholeness.

Come to me. Get away with me and you'll recover your life. I'll show you how to take a real rest.

There are several times in the gospels where Jesus calls his disciples and others to 'come after' him. Here is the only mention in Scripture where Jesus offers the invitation 'come to me'. That uniqueness should cause us to sit up and take notice. Peterson builds on other translations which simply read 'I will give you rest', but the way *The Message* expands on those words very much highlights what we have been saying so far in our journey. This is about life. Living full and free life. So rest is not just about redeeming time, buying it back from the marketplace; it is about recovering life and, as we have continually seen, being infused with the life of God.

The invitation to 'come to me' is offered to those who are tired, worn out and burned out; those who have become victims (through negligence, through weakness, or through their own deliberate fault) of the fast-paced, over-demanding world that we live in. It is they who need to rediscover in Jesus what real life and real rest look like.

How will you respond to this invitation? Will you hear the words, thinking how good it sounds, imagining a different way, and then walk away straight back to the marketplace and your normal patterns of work? Doing so will carry with it a risk, as does any time we hear the words of Jesus and choose to walk away.

Walk with me and work with me — watch how I do it. Learn the un-forced rhythms of grace. I won't lay anything heavy or ill-fitting on you. Keep company with me and you'll learn to live freely and lightly.

The NRSV translates these words as follows:

Take my yoke upon you, and learn from me; for I am gentle and humble in heart, and you will find rest for your souls. For my yoke is easy, and my burden is light.

In his commentary on Matthew, Wilkins describes the yoke as 'a common metaphor in Judaism for the law'.[17] If the law can be simplified to simply mean 'teaching' or 'instruction' or 'the way', then it changes what we see Jesus' meaning to be in these words. He is wanting us to take his teaching, his instruction and his way onto ourselves, and to find that this way is far better fitting for us than the burdens we are carrying. Rather than the relentless grind of busyness, Jesus offers us the opportunity to learn the 'unforced rhythms of grace'. Not slaves to our own self-destructive patterns, or a religiously legalistic system, but free to live freely and lightly.

Learning from Jesus is so much more than simply copying what he does. It is far more than just mimicking his rest. In a very real sense it is allowing him to creatively transform his life in us, to infuse his life within us, so that we can truly live as those who God has created us to uniquely be.

This way of life, though, however appealing, is offensive to the culture we live in today. It encourages us to seek who we are through what we do. Here Jesus' words are that we are to find ourselves and our true life not in the culture of our day, but in him. To take up his invitation is to say no to that culture, and as Robin Meyers says, to 'establish a community of alternative commitments and social practices'.[18]

Here lies the paradox: that it is this revolutionary stand against the cultures of our day that we find neither easy nor light, but that is the only way that true rest and freedom can be found.

Holy Saturday – Keeping the Sabbath?

To close this part of our journey exploring Jesus and rest, I want to enter into one of the truly sacred spaces of our Christian calendar, Holy Saturday. As nonconformists we have not always entered into this special day with the worship it deserves, instead simply skipping on to the joyful sunrise of Easter day. However, it has been a day that Bex and I have marked in our ministry from the beginning because this is a day where most of us will spend at least part of our lives, in the place of 'in-between'. God has acted at the cross, pouring out his love in a total, free and redemptive act of self-giving for the other, and God will act again as the sun breaks over the horizon on Sunday morning and the Son breaks free from the tomb. But Saturday?! A blank page in the most important story in human history. As Pete Greig emotively puts it in his book *God on Mute*, on this day there is 'no sound but the buzzing of flies around the corpse of the Son'.[19]

This is the place of unanswered questions, of deathly silence, and perhaps even rest?

I have deliberately not touched on the subject of death as rest in this book, because I think it would be a subject all on its own. However, for a moment it is worth noting that even here in the tomb, where it seems as if all hope is lost, where we cannot see what God is doing, when all the purposes and goals of God for the cosmos seem to have come to nothing – God is here. There is an old homily for Holy Saturday which begins: 'Something strange is happening – there is a great silence on earth today, a great silence and stillness. The whole earth keeps silent because the King is asleep.'[20]

When presiding over a burial I often find myself looking at what is inscribed on people's tombstones. You can tell a lot about the spiritual pulse of the general public by looking at what is written here in stone, perhaps too personal to speak about in life, but in death displayed for all to see. By far the most common phrase, no matter the belief, background or circumstance, is 'Rest in Peace'. There is something in our national psyche that associates death with rest.

Yet death in and of itself is not rest. Tom Smail writes that 'death is the collapse of all relationships into unresponsiveness'.[21] He continues 'All that makes up life is lost to the dead and they are lost to it.'[22] This is far from what we have spoken about as rest being infused with the life of God. If this was all there was to say about death, then of course we would be a hopeless people, but this is *not* all we are to say about it.

Firstly, the rest that can validly be spoken about after this life is the one in which we are held in love in the very presence of God. It is the moment when we experience in all its fullness and glory, the life of God, and we are infused with it to such a degree that it breaks us free even from the chains of death, as it did with Christ. This rest is not a fading out into the seemed peace of nothingness, but is the coming alive in the living relatedness of the one who brings life to everything.

In October 2018, Eugene Peterson died at the age of 85. Often referred to as 'the pastor's pastor', his writings and ministry have shaped millions around the world, including me. When I was reading the statement released by his family, I was struck by these words:

> It feels fitting that his death came on a Monday, the day of the week he always honoured as a Sabbath during his years as a pastor. After a lifetime of faithful service to the church – running the race with gusto – it is reassuring to know that Eugene has now entered into the fullness of the Kingdom of God and has been embraced by eternal Sabbath.

Peterson, with all those who came before him, has entered into the fullness of relationship with God through Christ.

Secondly, because Jesus enters this place of death, even here we know that God is present; even in this darkness we know that there is no place where his love cannot reach down.

Maybe here, as the stone rolls over the tomb on Friday, not to be moved until Sunday, the Son of God keeps the Sabbath. He rests. Not slipping into unresponsiveness, but held within the deep love and purpose of God. This mysterious Sabbath rest is honoured as a foretaste of a greater life, a deeper reality that is yet to be fulfilled, not just on Sunday, but through the ages and into the life to come.

Much like the mourners of Holy Saturday, we wait for that day. Our waiting, though, comes not at the tomb, but in the ordinariness of our own lives. As we seek to live this God-infused life in our places of work, our families, our churches and in any place our feet may step, we must do so with the knowledge that often, more often than we care to admit, we feel the strain.

8

Feeling the Strain

Each time you set a healthy boundary to rest, you say yes to more freedom and life.

I am hoping that we have now established in journeying through Scripture, that rest is not just an important 'slot in when you can' extra to life, but that it is integral for our lives as a means through which we connect with and receive the life of God.

Were we to live simply on the pages of this book then that realisation might be enough, but at some point we have to close these pages, or the pages of Holy Scripture, and we have to enter again into 'the real world'. This is a world full of joys and pleasures, but also one of challenges and demands.

It is right, then, that we take a moment to acknowledge the challenge that we face in putting some of what we have seen into practice. This is something that I am convinced most people struggle with, otherwise perhaps you would not have picked up this book.

I think back to the men's prayer breakfast I mentioned earlier. One of the questions I asked those who attended was around why we struggle with keeping the Sabbath command-ment. Most of us, if we were asked by our employers to com-mit murder, would say no. The same would be true if we were asked to commit adultery, and the same hopefully for stealing. However, if we were asked to work without rest on a regular basis, we would put that down to being 'just part of the job'. My question to these guys was: 'Why?' The command is still the same; in fact, as we have already seen, more is written about this command than any of the others. So why do we seem rel-atively OK with breaking it?

One of the answers that came back was telling. 'When we commit murder, or adultery, then the impact on society is easy to see. That just isn't there when we break the Sabbath.'

Therein lies the problem. Because we can't always see it, or because the ramifications are hidden, we assume that there is no problem. Many of us are literally choosing death over life day after day, week after week, for ourselves, our families and our faith, and we don't even see it. What we feel, though, are the symptoms of those choices.

Maybe you are aware of symptoms in your life, which you have never consciously attributed to a lack of rest, but as we have journeyed together you have yearned for something deeper. Perhaps you're still on the fence, but you know that the symptoms you experience in your life cannot be ignored any longer.

As we move through this chapter I hope that we can iden-tify some of the common struggles we face when we are una-ble or refuse to rest, because in acknowledging them, we have begun the first step to changing the environment and culture of our lives to be more susceptive to God's life, or as we saw in the story at the beginning, we will be tuning our ear to hear his life.

State Protected Rest?

Prior to 1994, Sunday trading was not generally allowed in the UK, with only a handful of shops legally allowed to open on Sundays. However, a bill went through Parliament in 1994 which enabled small shops to open without restriction on Sundays, and larger shops for no more than six consecutive hours between 10 a.m. and 6 p.m.

There were several groups that were opposed to the legislation, fearing that workers' rights and family life would be affected, as well as the loss of Sunday as a special day of rest. The campaign against the bill was called 'Keep Sunday Special'.

I was 10 years old in 1994, and so don't remember the change all that well, but my grandmother (whose age I shall leave out!) remembers it well.

She remembers at Easter in particular, when you would walk through town in the afternoon and there would be nothing open. She speaks about the peace of those moments, without the rush of the world around you going about its seeming normal busyness. She remembers that this all changed when Sunday trading began. Suddenly Sunday became like any other day, at least to the general population. Even though it seemed to many like a small change, to those who had known the rest that had been before, it felt anything but small.

There was also a fear that in the years to come, this would snowball into general unrestricted opening hours on a Sunday, which caused businesses to share concerns with the government of the day about the possible effects this would have over time.

A survey taken in 2014 stated that 72 per cent of people wanted to be able to have the freedom to shop whenever they desired and wanted Sunday trading to be unrestricted. There is always a need to balance progress and convenience against rights and freedoms. For many, Sunday is a special day, a Sabbath day when they want to be free to rest without the pressure of work. Sabbath rest is also about the rights of the workers to be able to rest without requirement to work continuously. Where should the balance lie between those two views? There are some who would frame this within the ever-present battle between traditionalism and progress, between the culture we have had in the past and the one that is being shaped now. Whether you agree with it or not, what is clear is that the concept of dedicated periods of rest is one that is increasingly being forgotten nationally.

There are those who would say, it is simply about my freedom to shop when I want, and that this does not affect anyone else. However, if I want to shop on a Sunday, then there has to be staff in the store to serve me and deliveries to those stores for stocks to be maintained, and transport links in the city such as buses and trains need to keep running. Cafés and restaurants will open longer because of the increased volume of people on a Sunday, and all this comes simply from my desire to shop. Now, there is nothing wrong with shopping in and of itself. I would even go as far as to say, and I know that some would disagree, that there is nothing wrong with shopping on a Sunday. The problem for me is the strain on the lives of individuals and society when we lose the importance of a designated day of rest. Whether that day comes on Monday, Tuesday, Wednesday, Thursday, Friday, Saturday or Sunday in many ways does not matter. What matters is that, in losing it from our collective life, we have increased the strain on our society, and that is hard to relieve.

The Forgotten Off-Switch

Most of us lead busy lives, but it prompts us to ask the question: 'Has it always been this way?' The answer is both yes and no. Yes, people have always been busy; there were busy people 2,000 years ago, 500 years ago, seventy-five years ago. Being busy is not a purely modern phenomenon. The 'no' comes when we recognize that the strain of busy that we experience today is unlike anything we have seen before. Technology has had an impact on our day-to-day lives like no other time in our human history. We find it very hard to switch off.

In his book *90,000 Hours*, Rodney Green gives an enlightening statistic that CEOs of UK companies spend on average 14.5 hours per day, 6.5 days per week on their job. Ninety-five hours per week. He scrutinizes this statistic, saying: 'Few of those working 70+ hours per week are embarrassed by the culture they are helping to create: on the contrary, they wear it like a badge of achievement.'[1]

This is a trap that I have fallen into in ministry. It is so easy to look at the hours you have worked and to assume that because you have worked for a large amount of time that you are being more productive. It gives you a measureable figure with which to evaluate and appraise your time.

Now this is not a simple black and white issue, and I am not simply saying that if you work less it will go away. Part of the problem here is that our identity is so hung up on what we do that it feeds this unhealthy cycle. How much we work is really just the means through which we measure it. So if your value and identity is totally invested in your work, then the more you work the more valuable you are. Eventually, working more hours becomes the means of maintaining your value, whilst never really experiencing the freedom and identity of simply 'being'.

In a world dominated by technology, we are acting increasingly like machines. If I want a machine to produce more, I simply run it for longer, but the danger lies when we start treating ourselves in this way. We start to think that in order to be more productive, to produce more, to accumulate more value, we simply have to run ourselves for longer periods of time. The problem of course is, as we have already discovered, that we were not designed that way. We are not machines.

We will explore the impact that this has on our mental health in a moment, but clearly the view that a lack of regular rest does not have an impact on society, either collectively or individually, is reaching the realms of indefensible.

Technology has done many wonderful things for us. It has enabled us to talk to relatives on the other side of the world. It allows us to gain access to information that previously only the learned and powerful could peruse. It helps us to treat more diseases and improve the quality of life of millions. It will be the means in the future for us to combat climate change and, in doing so, once again take seriously our call to be caretakers of the world that God has made. In so many ways it has enhanced our lives. However, it has not come without a price. Technology is not a universal good because it is used by human beings and, as such, can exacerbate our flaws as well as highlight our strengths. Speaking about technology being readily accessible wherever we are, Alex Soojung-Kim Pang, a researcher at the Institute for the Future in Silicon Valley, says:

> The digital dream was that it would allow us to break our eight hour workday into several 'chunks'. If in the middle of the day, you needed to go off and do childcare, you could come back and work later. That isn't happening. Instead, those 'chunks' of work have been ground down to a fine powder that settles over our entire waking hours.[2]

We are never switched off. How often is my phone the first thing I look at in the morning? More often than I would like. Even social media, which as Bishop Curry said at the Royal Wedding recently, allows us to 'socially be dysfunctional'[3] with one another, is part of our problem. I have almost one hundred 'friends' on Facebook, which is fairly low as far as an average goes, I think. Now this basically means that there are almost one hundred people whose lives I see updates from on my phone every day. Almost one hundred people that I, consciously or subconsciously, compare my life to every day. I don't have to spend hours hunting this information down, or even interact with these people at all, it is readily at hand on my phone.

Modern life is overwhelming. With all the demands and pressures we face, our relationship to time has never been more warped and in need of redeeming. Dr Hart highlights this broken relationship:

> On one hand, we think of it as the 'enemy', so we're always trying to 'beat the clock' as if time were against us. On the other hand, we almost seem to worship time. We place big clocks on tall steeples where we can all stare at them, then attach large bells that can clang to the hours to remind us how little we are accomplishing.[4]

A friend of ours is a holistic therapist in Devon, and she brought my attention to her blog, where she was discussing insomnia, and how the majority of people she treats struggle with sleep problems. She speaks of how 90 per cent of the aromatherapy blends she makes for clients include an oil to support good sleep and address the problem of insomnia.

When it comes to our discussion on time, one thing stands out in her blog that I had not thought about before, which is the disruption to our patterns of rest caused by Daylight Savings Time.

Daylight Savings Time is something that industrialized countries in the mid-latitudes have embraced in the past century enabling them to accommodate different spheres of work with their culture. Most of us will go to work around the same time each day, and our children will have the same school hours each day. As we have already discussed, we run to the clock, whatever the season. If you are from an agrarian sphere of work, then when the sun rises and sets, and how much daylight you need to get your work done, matters. So it was thought that we can gain an hour at the end of the day in the summer months when daylight lasts longer by setting our clocks an hour later.

However, according to a BBC Radio 4 programme with Matthew Walker, a neuroscientist and director of the Centre for Human Sleep Science, it is not without its challenges. My friend writes: 'Walker talks in terms of epidemic and catastrophe when discussing this modern and cultural problem of sleep deprivation, weighted by alarming facts such as a 24% increase in heart attacks when the clocks go forward and we lose an hour's sleep, and respectively a decrease of 21% in the autumn when we claim that hour back.'[5]

It does seem as though our strange relationship with time, and our desire to change it in order to suit our purpose, is not without its costs, or cause of strain.

We have previously looked at redeeming time, or buying back time from the marketplace, which in today's marketplace is more needed than ever. We do not simply need a healthier balance between work and rest, but we need to restructure and reset our patterns of living to be reorientated towards that which brings us life; that which infuses the life of God into our very being; to find rest not just as recovery but as foundational. Pang cautions us 'Too often we treat rest as either a diversion, or a luxury that we do once we're finished with everything else. The problem these days is we're never finished with everything else'.[6]

In order to do that we need to set boundaries. In my previous church I worked six days a week but worked a pattern that I was increasingly aware was unhealthy for me. When I moved to my current post, I said to the leadership team during the interview phase that I needed to work a five-day week, and that I was convinced that I would be more productive working five days per week than six. That has very much turned out to be the case. I have taken the time to rest well, and that has had an impact across my whole life, including my work.

Taking the time to rest is not so much about 'switching off'. Each time you set a healthy boundary to rest, you say yes to more freedom and life. It is both a switching off and a switching on. You are switching off to that which has dominated and switching on to the life that can be found in rest. Your no to endless work is a yes to a fuller and deeper sense of life.

It might be that on your rest day, or rest times, you need to turn off your phone? Some people take the step of turning off all technology, and this may or may not be something you want to do. The issue with our phones, and I know this is true for me, is that it means I am accessible to everyone who has my number at any moment, and I have literally the distraction of a world of information that stops me engaging with the people right in front of me. Perhaps we need a Sabbath rest not simply from the technology, but from our inability at times to switch off.

Mental Health in the Trenches

Our struggle to switch off has more repercussions for us than simply feeling overtired or busy. Dr Hart starkly reminds us '"Hurry sickness" is a killer'.[7]

One of the most encouraging things I have seen in recent times has been an increase in awareness of mental health issues. Not only is the awareness of and understanding for those who have mental illness improving, but so is our understanding that we all need to take our mental health seriously. The mind is beautifully complex, powerful and yet painfully fragile. When we keep pushing ourselves to keep going, stopping rarely, if ever, then we begin to feel the strain mentally.

As part of the preparation for writing this book, I surveyed 250 people across the age spectrum, people of faith and none, male and female, from all around the UK, and I asked them eight basic questions about rest.

One of the interesting things was that when the results were in, although 65 per cent said that they felt that they had a healthy balance between work and rest in their lives, the symptoms that they experienced when they didn't rest well were clear:

Seventy-three per cent experienced higher irritability.
Sixty-three per cent said they felt lethargic.
Sixty per cent experienced a noticeably lower mood.
Fifty-three per cent had trouble sleeping.

When asked what some of the other symptoms they experienced due to a lack of rest were, the following kept coming up:

Lack of creativity.
Destructive coping strategies.
Anxiety.
Mood swings.
Depressed.
Stressed.
Muscle spasms.

These symptoms were distributed fairly evenly across those who answered the question of whether they had a healthy work and rest balance. What we can see from this is that whether you feel you have a healthy balance between work and rest in your life or not, we each need to make sure we are self-aware enough to spot when we need to redress the balance.

Much like the body, the mind cannot keep going under strain for too long and needs time to rest. 'The human frame has its limits, and we should build into our lives adequate rest and recovery times so as to allow for healing and restoration to take place.'[8]

Issues of mental health will affect all of us at some point in our lives in the same way that physical health issues will. This is part of who we are as human beings. And just as we need to make sure that we look after our physical bodies, and are aware of symptoms that will let us know that something is wrong, so we need to do the same with our mental health.

Christians are not immune from the challenges surrounding mental health in the same way that we are not immune from getting physically sick. Yet in the same way that there is a stigma in society about mental health, the same is true within the church, perhaps more so. Very often Christians do not know how to process depression or anxiety, and burnout is a sign that you are 'working hard for the kingdom'.

In a previous post I had a period of high stress that led to mild depression, and I remember a member of the congregation coming up to me and saying, 'I didn't think ministers struggled with those kinds of things.'

Firstly, let me say that I think that this was a comment expressing genuine surprise, not a critical one. Secondly, let me give you the answer that I gave her: 'Yes, we do!'

As Christians we must be aware of the need to treat mental health seriously. In our churches we need to make sure that we set realistic patterns of work for our staff and volunteers and make sure that even when resources are low, we promote, plan for, and if needs be insist on, days off, and time off being taken.

In our home groups we need to make sure that we take people's sharing of stress and anxiety seriously without belittling it. We need to challenge unhealthy work practices, if necessary, and encourage positive ones where rest and Sabbath play an important part. This will be a challenge within our current western evangelical church culture: 'Those brought up in a tradition that we should always be up and doing, or on the frankly muscular Christianity of some schools, may find it hard to see that we must come apart and rest awhile to get stress into proportion.'[9]

Asking for help when we are not coping is vitally important! There have been times when I have had to sit down with Bex and look at coping strategies, working patterns and rest periods. Let me put it as bluntly as this: if you reach a point where you are not coping, you will either seek help and be able to manage the situation, or you will not seek help and the situation will manage you, but it will come to a head at some time. It is not always easy to ask for help. A very important factor is our early histories. A defining period of my life was the time between when my biological father died and my mum remarried. During this time I didn't have a father, and the earliest memory of fatherhood I have was not having one in school when everyone else did. The most constant male figure in my life before my mum remarried was my grandfather, who had been in the navy since the age of 16 and was very much of the opinion that to show emotion or to ask for help was a weakness. Even from a young age this was the message that was pushed onto me that this is what masculinity looked like, and it wasn't until years later, when I had some counselling about something else, that this came out as an important issue.

How does rest come in? Regular rest is an important way that God's life is brought into the places of death in our lives, in a healing way. In order to make this a reality, though, we have to be willing to see it, to own it, and challenge the view that we must keep going at all costs; at the cost of our mental health and sanity.

According to mental health charity Mind, 'relaxation is the natural answer to stress. Everyone should make time in the day to relax, whether we feel under stress, or not.'[10] The charity go on to talk about the difference between relaxation and recreation, and that even doing pleasurable activities can make us feel more stressed: 'trying to relax by doing even more is not the answer.'[11]

Burnout

This morning I went to get a cup of coffee before sitting down to write, and noticed in this particular shop a drinks flask with the slogan 'Rise & Grind'. And that summed up for me part of the culture that many experience, the day-to-day grind of life. If we keep going without stopping, if we fail to switch off, if we ignore the signs of strain to our mental and physical health, then the dangers we face are very real. One of the very real dangers is burnout. Burnout left unchecked can lead us to a negative spiral that will threaten our health and relationships as well as our work:

Whilst our work and accomplishments do not form the basis of our acceptance with God, they can provide us with a strong sense of confidence and wellbeing. When this is reduced, it inevitably leads to frustration, as we work harder to overcome a sense of guilt that our motives and achievements are not good; this also leads to a crippling loss of perspective that sees everything as waste and failure. The downward spiral can seem out of control.[12]

The British evangelist Christmas Evans once said, 'I'd rather burn out than rust out in the service of the Lord.'[13] The problem I have found in ministry, and as I have spoken to other ministers (and the same I am sure is true for those in other Christian roles) is that this view is far more common than we would care to admit. The demands of ministry seem at times to be endless. There is always another sermon to write, another person to visit, another meeting to attend, another strategy session to plan. I know that many others in different roles are just as busy as I am, but the challenge I have always found is that often with vocational roles your identity can so easily be wrapped up in what you do. This was never the case when I worked for an insurance company when I was younger. I left the office at the end of the day and the work stayed there. I genuinely think that in my time working there I did not give what happened in that office much thought at all when I went home. It was simply what I did, which left plenty of time to rest and relax and build and maintain relationships.

However, in ministry this has been a constant challenge because vocational work is about who you are. You don't just work in a care profession, you are a carer. If this is who I am, then what are the boundaries of self-care that will enable me to express this in a way that does not take over my life?

When we feel as though our tiredness or stress has developed into burnout, we need to take action. Peter Brain speaks about how he took a trip with his wife on the coastal road between San Francisco and Los Angeles. There were regular lay-bys or 'turnout bays' along the way which meant that they could pull out of traffic, take a moment to pause and to look at the beautiful view. Without these lay-bys they would have only been able to take passing glances at the scenery without the space to fully appreciate and enjoy it.

Life has many beautiful sights to be appreciated and enjoyed. As we glance back to our journey through Genesis, we remember that God has created a world that is 'very good', one which is to be enjoyed. He has given us loving relationships. He has given us work. However, sometimes it is easy to just exist within the flow of traffic and never really take the time to stop and look. When we drive out of Bath towards the M4 motorway there is a wonderful view out over the valley and rolling hills, and on every occasion I glance to my right and try to admire it without crashing on the winding road. Never have I pulled the car over to take time, even a moment, to really appreciate it.

What are the lay-bys or turnout bays in your life? Where are the moments when you can stop, take time and appreciate all that life has to bring to you? Where are the moments when you can breathe the air and feel connected to the world and people around you in a fresh way? Where are the moments that God's life is being infused into yours?

These moments are ones that are aside from our regular 'days off' or Sabbaths, but are moments that punctuate our time with God's life. These moments are part of the way that we are saved from burnout, and part of the way if we are experiencing it that we can redress the imbalance. Burnout or rust out? Surely there is a better way? Brain quotes James Berkeley who, reflecting on Paul's comments about running the race in Acts 20, says: 'I want neither to burn out nor rust out. I want to finish the race.'[14]

Don't burn out. Take time, rest on the journey, be infused with life, and finish the race!

9

You're Worth It

How do we make choices each and every day that are based on a
healthy self-love which is reflective of God's love for us?

Having seen the strain that a lack of rest puts us under, it is
important to turn our attention to what we can do about it. We
do not simply do this because we want to avoid the negative
results of that strain, although at the beginning that might be
a motivation for many. This is like those who come to faith
through fear of hell. It is not so much that this isn't a valid and
real route into faith, but that at some point there needs to be a
deeper connection, a reaching out to and receiving of life. So
when we think about rest, we will never truly benefit from the
life God has to offer us in rest, or be infused with it, until we
understand that it is life that he is offering, not simply a get-
out-of-jail-free card for burnout.

So it is important to start this chapter by asking, why self-
care? If there are many around the world who work long hours,
or two jobs, or many jobs, and feel the strain and keep on

going, why bother to stop? Even if we have established that Holy Scripture testifies to the importance of rest, how is it important to *me*? To *you*?

Your Value to God

We can become used to words and be so familiar with them that they lose something of their impact and meaning for us. This is no different for us on our faith journey as any other walk of life, which is why, when giving instructions to the church about communion, the apostle Paul encourages them not to 'let familiarity breed contempt'.[1]

Perhaps a phrase that we say a lot to ourselves and to others falls into this category: 'God loves you.' You may be sat there thinking, 'I already know that', and I hope that's true, but the heart of what Paul is saying is that just because you know it doesn't mean that you don't need to be struck with fresh awe and wonder by it regularly.

God loves you! Let's think back over our journey so far.

The one who created all that is seen and unseen, the one who uttered a word and everything was, who held the boundaries of the land and sea apart, who set the sun and the planets and the stars in the sky. This God loves *you*!

The one whose love for you is not merely expressed in sentiment but in revealing a 'way' in which you can live to experience full and free life. This God loves *you*!

The one who sends his one and only Son into the world to show you the full extent of his love, and who continually calls you to experience that love and rest: 'Come to me, all you that are weary and are carrying heavy burdens, and I will give you rest.'[2] This God loves *you*!

As small as you may seem, as unlikely as it may sound, as far removed from what you knew as it might seem, there is a simple truth that, if we grasp it, will blow our minds. Woven into the fabric of the cosmos, stitched into time and space, imprinted in the very fibres of every living thing in existence, is the beating heart of creation itself: God loves *you*!

The reason why I mention this in this chapter is that when you truly know you are loved and valued, you will start to treat yourself as valuable. Rest will become an extension and expression of God's love for you. It is to delight and be delighted in. Dan Allender reflects:

'The Sabbath is our play day – not as a break from the routine of work, but as a feast that celebrates the superabundance of God's creative love to give glory for no other reason other than Love himself loves to create.'[3]

It would be very easy for us to treat this gift of rest like any other commandment. To do this, even off the back of being birthed in love, would be to mimic the religious leaders of Jesus' day. They too would have thought their foundation was firm, and their motives good. Grace and legalism are only one human heartbeat away from each other, and when grace itself becomes legalistic, that is the most tragic thing of all.

When the gift that is given to remove our burden and bring us freedom ends with us putting on again the heavy chains of slavery, then we have lost sight not only of the gift but of the giver.

Paul writes to the church in Ephesus: 'But God, who is rich in mercy, out of the great love with which he loved us even when we were dead through our trespasses, made us alive together with Christ . . .'[4]

It is because of God's great love for us that he longs for us to be infused with his life, to be brought into the fullness of the life he has for us. You are worth that love, and that life, not because of anything you have done, or not done, but because of who he is. The one who is perfect love sent his Son to die and rise again, and because of this we can know life even in our places of death.

There is a particular make-up brand that advertises with the slogan 'because you're worth it'. Essentially that is the strapline that comes attached to God's rest for us: because you're worth it! Or, as my wife wrote in her journal, whilst she was exploring the spiritual exercises in forty days of silence, '[God said] you've done the hard work of the week already, so now I just want you to marvel at my love for u. Just marvel and watch my love for u unfold. Welcome to Rest!'

The Importance of Self-care

[L]ove your neighbor as yourself.[5]

We cannot truly love our neighbour unless we love ourselves. However, for some people this is one of the most difficult things to do. We might be able to get on board with the idea that God loves us, and we might even love ourselves in a general sense, but how do we make choices each and every day that are based on a healthy self-love which is reflective of God's love for us? How do we make the choices every day to care for ourselves, and by doing so, experience deeper life not just for us, but those around us?

This is not always easy. We don't find it very easy to be vulnerable, not just with others but with ourselves, yet that vulnerability lies at the heart of the gospel. We see that in Paul's incredible words to the church in Philippi:

Let the same mind be in you that was in Christ Jesus,
who, though he was in the form of God,

did not regard equality with God
as something to be exploited,
but emptied himself,
taking the form of a slave,
being born in human likeness.
And being found in human form,
he humbled himself
and became obedient to the point of death –
even death on a cross.[6]

There is great vulnerability in the incarnation, where a God of limitless power takes on the limitations of humanity. Richard Rohr reflects poignantly: 'It's amazing: Christianity is the only religion that dares to call God a lamb. And nevertheless we've spent two thousand years avoiding vulnerability.'[7]

Part of our self-care means we have to honestly take a look within ourselves and be willing to be vulnerable. Be willing to admit that we are struggling. Be willing to admit that we might need help. There may have been others who have already pointed out to us that we are doing too much, or we need to learn to rest better. Perhaps we have listened, tried, struggled and fallen back into old patterns. Perhaps we have tried to carry on and block those voices out. We know best, right? The problem I have found, though, is that I do not know best. Left to my own devices my self-care can be, and has been, woeful. I need to be open and vulnerable, with myself, with others and with God, the one who alone does not get worn out:

Have you not known? Have you not heard?
The LORD is the everlasting God,
the Creator of the ends of the earth.
He does not faint or grow weary;

his understanding is unsearchable.
He gives power to the faint,
and strengthens the powerless.
Even youths will faint and be weary,
and the young will fall exhausted;
but those who wait for the LORD shall renew their strength,
they shall mount up with wings like eagles,
they shall run and not be weary,
they shall walk and not faint.[8]

Constantly in the struggle for clear boundaries and valuable self-care I am reminded of those words, 'Have you not known? Have you not heard? The LORD is the everlasting God, the Creator of the ends of the earth. He does not faint or grow weary . . .' *He* does not. I do, but he does not. So it is his rest that I must enter, it is on him that I must wait.

However, that does not mean that there are not things that I need to do in order to care for myself well.

Buying Back Time from the Marketplace

For those that work, the daily grind of employment can be one of the main areas where we need to buy back time from. This will enable us to invest that time in other areas and to enjoy the rest that God gives us.

What are your patterns of rest when it comes to work? It can be one of the hardest places to build a healthy pattern and rhythm. When it comes to rest in the workplace, it might not always look like what you expect.

For example, if you work in a profession that means that you are on your feet all day, or quite physically active, then rest might look like taking a moment to sit down. On the other hand, if you are in a profession where you spend most of your time at a desk, or fairly inactive, then rest from that 'normality' might be taking a moment to stand up and walk around.

What we need to do is to think about the environment we are in, think about what our daily routine might look like, and then think about how we are most likely to experience rest in that environment. Even walking to make a drink can be a moment of refreshing in more ways than one.

It is for each of us to be self-aware enough to not only be realistic about our work schedule and environment, but also about how we would best experience that rest.

A great workplace example of buying back time is from my friend and colleague Nigel, who is the chaplaincy team leader at the University of Bath. Sometimes when I send Nigel an email, I get an automated response roughly saying this: 'Thank you for writing. I am away today (*date*). I will pick emails up this evening. I will not normally reply for 48 hours (*1st class post reply time*) to non-urgent emails, to enable a considered response. Please email again if a more rapid reply is required.'

What I really like about Nigel's approach is that he is literally buying back time to give a considered and measured response. Emails are one of the real challenges of a working day, mainly because they arrive instantly and we feel as though they require an instant response. How many times per day do you check your emails? Does the mailbox you use ever close?

One of the ways in which you can buy back time in the workplace is to limit the amount of times you check your email. Don't leave the program open all the time, try checking it only once per day, around the time the snail-mail is delivered. Treat it like literal post. Just because it is electronic does not mean that it is more important. If you can't get down to once per day, then try morning and afternoon. It might not seem like much, but even the smallest gains can lead to big results. I remember reading an interview with the head of British cycling, Sir Dave Brailsford, who was talking about how they had become so successful at the Olympic Games in 2008 and 2012. They had adopted a programme of 'marginal gains'. Brailsford said in the interview: 'We searched for small improvements everywhere and found countless opportunities. Taken together, we felt they gave us a competitive advantage.'[9]

Changes that might seem small in themselves, when you build them together with others, can make a big difference.

Rhythms of Rest

Having thought briefly about rest patterns in our work, let's think a little bit more about routine because it is a great way to establish a pattern of rest and buy time back from the marketplace.

When we think about Genesis, we see that God created the world with rhythms and patterns, which happen without us noticing, but which enrich all life in the cosmos. We are part of this great cosmic rhythm, but we also have the God-given ability to shape the rhythm and pattern of our lives too.

I have already mentioned that when I took up my post here in Bath I had a conversation with the leaders about my working pattern. In order for me to be refreshed, and to have a sustainable ministry, I needed to make sure that I had a pattern of work that worked for me.

Daily

One of the ways that I have found rhythm in my day is to split the day into three sections.

I mentioned back in Chapter Five that this was something really helpful that came out of my ministerial training. What I then make sure I do is only work two out of those three sessions. So if I know that I have an evening meeting, then I will either take the morning or the afternoon off. This way I am making sure that I am getting a period of rest each day, where I can give quality time to my family.

Another rhythm I have found is taking a break to go and make a drink. When I am working for longer periods in my study, I try to go and make a drink each hour, or hour and a half. Not only does it give me a break from my surroundings, force me to stand up and move around, but I often bump into people and have a moment of conversation which can also be refreshing, although it does depend on who I bump into!

Speaking of drinks, can I encourage you to think about what I challenged people in my previous church to do when boiling the kettle? Whilst the kettle is boiling, don't use the time to go away and do something else, but simply pause, be still, settle yourself. A kettle takes around two minutes to boil, but those two minutes, a couple of times per day, could be a means through which you get a moment of rest.

Another daily rhythm is taking my lunch break. Sometimes there is a temptation to bring lunch back to my desk and to work through whilst eating. There have certainly been times when I've done this, and times when I have genuinely needed to do so. But wherever possible I try to take my lunch break away from my study.

One of the ways that I have found rhythm in my week is my regular days off.

Having worked before with one day off, and having worked several years now with two, I can tell you that I am far more productive than I have been before. I am more present to those I visit pastorally, I am able to craft time to think strategically about vision and mission, I am able to put more energy into the things I do.

The great challenge has come in realizing that this rest is not something I earn or justify through my productivity, it is a gift from God that I might more fully experience his life. Even when I am less productive than I would hope, this rest is still a vital part of who I am.

What has been really helpful is to have consistently had the same days off in my time here in Bath. I take Friday and Saturday as my days off, and the congregation know that on these days I am not around unless there is an emergency. I am blessed in that the congregation are respectful of this and my rest is not filled with eternal pressure from the church about coming back to do one thing or another, which I know some of my colleagues in other churches find to be the case.

Another rhythm for my week has come in how often I am out of an evening. When we moved to Bath Bex was pregnant with Leo, and I knew that life after his birth would look very different to how it did when we first arrived. I was determined to have a weekly rhythm that could transition into parenthood without me having to suddenly pull back from half the things I was doing. We made the decision that I would not be out more evenings a week than I was in. That gave me a maximum of three evenings out, including Sunday, and four evenings in.

I chose from the start to give priority to my family, to my self-care and to rest. I remember a quote I heard years ago from Robert Murray McCheyne, who said that God had given him the gospel and a horse. He had worn out the horse and could no longer preach the gospel.[10] We are of no use to those we love and care for, and less use to the gospel, if we work ourselves to exhaustion.

Monthly

One of the ways I have found rhythm in my month is through quiet days.

This gives me the space to be able to receive, to be still, to get out of the usual routine and pressure of working life. It gives me the ability to rest, in that it gives me the ability to be infused with God's life. For the first few years of my ministry in Bath I have driven the forty-five minutes to Glastonbury and spent time at Abbey House, a retreat house which is part of the diocese of Bath and Wells. At the end of 2017 the house closed, which was a real loss to those of us who had found there a place of refreshing and rest, as well as the staff who had lost their jobs. Across the country at the moment there seem to be places like Abbey House closing on a regular basis; we have known three in our part of the country close in the last couple of years. In a time where people are increasingly bruised and broken from the marketplace and worn out from religion, these places of sanctuary are vitally important, and we lose them at great cost to our ministry and mission.

Another way I have found rhythm is through ecumenical prayer and worship events. To be able to come and receive is such an important part of rest for me. In my role I am often in the role of 'giver', especially when it comes to corporate worship and prayer. To be able to come and simply be still is a wonderful gift of life to me. I tend to vary where I go; there are no shortages of churches in Bath.

Annual

One of the ways I have found rhythm in my year is through retreats.

It is important to be able to lay myself into God's hands over a fuller amount of time. To hold before him my work, my relationships, my very self and to know that these things are held and sustained not by me trying to juggle them or maintain priorities; they are held ultimately by him.

Another rhythm has been making sure I use my annual leave entitlement. It is far too easy to think that the demands of ministry and the work of the kingdom means that I must work all the possible days God sends. And when we are sitting down to plan when we are taking our holiday, there is a tendency to feel twitchy when it falls when other events are on. What this twitchiness shows is that I do not always find it easy to trust that God holds these things together without me. I think that is a common problem for those in ministry. We might not be willing to admit it so readily, but our actions sometimes give us away. Yet, I have a 100 per cent record of returning from holiday to churches that have not collapsed, where the staff, leaders, volunteers and members have managed perfectly well in my absence. What I mean to say is, God is perfectly able to carry on his purpose whether I am in the building or not.

The annual leave entitlement you have is a gift! There are many throughout the world who do not enjoy that gift, or freedom, or right. Their work and labour are exploited and they often toil in unimaginable conditions. Those freedoms and rights were hard won for us, and they provide us with the gift of rest where we can genuinely connect with those around us and be infused with the life of God. Don't trade them away.

These rhythms have not come naturally, and in reality, some have come out of painful periods where the consequences of different patterns have been born. That might be the same for you. It might be that you have experienced the strain of life without rest, and that you know that from this pain needs to come a new pattern, a new rhythm. This intention is a wonderful thing, a holy moment, a moment of creation and life within us. We need to grasp hold of it and, by God's grace, help to form it into a new rhythm for our lives.

The rhythms that I have mentioned might not easily translate into your context. However, I do believe that the heart and intention behind them can translate across sectors and contexts and can lead us to develop patterns and rhythms that work for each of us.

This can take time. Researchers have said that it takes around two months to form a new habit. Depending on your starting point, it can take longer. However, forming that new habit, being proactive rather than reactive when it comes to rest, gives us a far better chance of seeing it take root in our lives. 'Because of the power of habit, it's easier to do something regularly and routinely rather than just when we feel like it or just when we can fit it in.'[11]

We need that intention to start a new habit, and a realization that what we are aiming for is worth the hard work in establishing it.

I was struck recently by the words of Eugene Peterson, in an article he wrote in 1981 for *The Leadership Journal* which would go on to form a chapter in his book *The Contemplative Pastor*.

I am busy because I am lazy. I indolently let other people decide what I will do instead of resolutely deciding myself. I let people who do not understand the work of the pastor write the agenda for my day's work because I am too slipshod to write it myself. But these people don't know what a pastor is supposed to do. The pastor is a shadow figure in their minds, a marginal person vaguely connected with matters of God and good will. Anything remotely religious or somehow well-intentioned can be properly assigned to the pastor.

Because these assignments to pastoral service are made sincerely, I lazily go along with them. It takes effort to refuse, and there's always the danger that the refusal will be interpreted as a rebuff, a betrayal of religion and a calloused disregard for people in need.[12]

We need to take control! I know that I have the freedom to plan my diary in a way that many others do not. I know that largely 90 per cent of what goes into my diary is because I have put it there. Even if you don't have that level of freedom in diary planning, you will have some, and it is important for you to take that freedom and allow it to help you shape a rhythm that will bring life to you.

In the previous chapter we saw that the stakes are high, but I hope we are seeing now that change is possible, and when change comes it can enliven us to depths of life and relationship that we didn't know we could find.

Buying Back Time for Relationship

The concept of buying back time is not simply that we can store it up, hidden away as if our mere lack of use of it was the goal for our resting. Sabbath and rest are not simply the absence of something but the presence of something deeper. We do not simply buy back time *from* the marketplace, but we buy back time *for*. For a moment I want to focus on what I have said earlier, that relationship is central to this idea of rest as being infused with God's life. How might we buy back time from the marketplace, *for* relationships?

Buying back time for God

Be still before the LORD, and wait patiently for him . . .[13]

God has created us in love for relationship and wants us to experience the fullness of his love and life. He is constantly communicating with us in ways we cannot begin to imagine, if we will only tune our ears to hear what he is saying to us. As Mark Buchanan reminds us: 'God is everywhere. God hovers in the air just behind you. God slips in, furtive and alert, among your comings and your goings. God listens, and watches, and – yes – speaks. Only, you need to slow down enough to notice.'[14]

So many times we go through life unaware of his presence because so much else drowns him out. The busyness is like the noise of the waves crashing on the shore of our lives, drowning out the gentle and quiet whisper that so often speaks the words 'come to me'. Often we become aware of him in the time of our need, but fail to realize our need for him each and every moment of the day, in work or in rest.

That call will frequently come from within. When Augustinian friar Benignus O'Rourke speaks about silent prayer, he speaks of hidden treasure, buried deep within us: 'While we are immersed in our daily lives, most of us are barely conscious of what we are thinking. But when we sit in God's presence I begin to see that

I have lived most of my life running away from myself. Losing myself in activities, in work, in diversion, I have lived outside myself.'[15]

Augustine puts it equally well: 'You were there before my eyes, but I had deserted even my own self, and I did not find the God of my own heart.'[16]

Do we hear God calling us, wooing us, drawing us in? Are we able to hear that beckoning? Will we be still enough to listen to him, to meet with him?

Each of us are the same in that we need God. When I put it like that it doesn't sound enough, really, but then our words so poorly convey our utter dependence on the one who is holding every quark of the cosmos together even at this moment.

There are two words for life that are mentioned in the New Testament. The first, '*bios*', means to literally be alive, which all living things have in common. It is from this word that we get our word 'biology'. The second is '*zoe*', which is the life God gives. *Zoe* is more than simply walking around breathing; it is about full, genuine and vigorous life, it is life that pulses through every part of you, not just your veins. It is this life that God wants us to experience, not just to be alive, but to live!

It caused St Patrick to pray famously:

Christ with me,
Christ before me,
Christ behind me,
Christ in me,
Christ beneath me,
Christ above me,
Christ on my right,
Christ on my left,
Christ when I lie down,

Christ when I sit down,
Christ when I arise,
Christ in the heart of every man who thinks of me,
Christ in the mouth of everyone who speaks of me,
Christ in every eye that sees me,
Christ in every ear that hears me.[17]

Because the noise of our busyness so often drowns out his speaking, or creates a haze through which it is hard to see him, it is important for us to take time, to buy back time in order to still ourselves and receive and be tuned into his full and free life. God through his Word encourages us so many times to 'be still', and it is not that activity is bad, but that there comes a time when in order to go deeper, connect deeper, we need to stop and wait and reconnect with our Maker. The American Bible teacher Margaret Feinberg once wrote: 'Sometimes you have to slow to a stop and reset before you can experience the divine presence. My hunger to know God increased as I learned to develop a healthy rhythm in life and rediscovered the wonder of rest.'[18]

We all have this need, but we will all express it differently, and connect with God differently. God has created you with a song in your heart, a song that only you can sing. You are unique and precious and valuable, and so it stands to reason that if God went through the effort to create you this way, then it would be part of the way he chooses to relate to you. If Moses had not been a curious man, perhaps he would not have stopped to notice the burning bush that was not consumed. But because God knew who he was, he knew how to get his attention. He knew how to draw him in.

So part of the way to buy back time for God, each day, each week, each month, each year, is to ask ourselves who he has created us to be. What song did he put in your heart? If nature makes your heart sing, then get out and experience him in the rest in creation. If it is people that make your sing, then experience him in the joy of rest in relationship. If it is silence and solitude that makes your heart sing, then experience and be enlivened by him in the stillness of silence. Do not be like anyone else. Be you – a 'you' that is no longer content to simply go about this world with just a pulse, but who really wants to live. That life is found uniquely and fully in the God who has created all things, and who looks at them and says that they are good. Make sure that your rest is one that connects with *him*.

Buying back time for those we love

All too often I know this to be true in my own life, that when we fail to rest, it is those around us who will also bear the cost. What I can end up offering them are the dregs of my time rather than the best of it. I think that I am offering them myself, but what I am actually offering them is a poor reflection of myself, a shell, a shadow. I am too tired to be fully present, I am too focused on what I need (rest) rather than their needs, and all of this impacts on the relationships I have. So buying back time from the marketplace gives us the ability to build, sustain and nurture relationships with the people in our lives. It gives us the ability to be able to offer the very best of ourselves to others.

David Murray speaks about marriage and asks a two-fold question: 'Would you accept a "successful" job (or ministry) at the cost of a happy marriage? If someone were to look at your calendar, would they know your answer to that question?'[19]

How do I show my family and friends that I love them? The list could be endless, and that is no bad thing at all. But what

I know is that if I am too worn down, burned out or exhausted to even pull out the list, let alone have the time to do anything on it, then my relationships will suffer.

However, when I have bought back time from the marketplace and invested it in my relationships, with Bex and Leo, then we can all experience a sense of God's life through our rest together. It is then that we are able to give the best gift of ourselves to each other.

I remember hearing someone tell their children that God has made us with a 'Sabbath DNA'. That God has wired the need to rest into our bodies and that we cannot simply keep going on and on without stopping. So a question that comes regarding rest and relationships is not only whether we will buy back time from the marketplace *for* our relationships, but whether we will buy back that time *in* our relationships? In other words, this is not something *I* do that I believe will benefit my family, but it is something *we* do because we believe that it mirrors something of God's way of being in the world that we want to experience together. That our family life does not simply co-exist as those who are alive, but thrives as those who go deep together so that we can truly live.

We often speak of time in terms of quality or quantity. We ask whether it is quality time or the quantity of time that is important. In my recent survey of 250 people, 83 per cent (more than 200 people) said that quality is more important than quantity when it comes to rest. This was one of the statistics that didn't surprise me, as in my experience most people go for the word 'quality' in questions like this. Quality of time is very important if we want to make sure that we give those who we love the best of ourselves. However, we should not use 'quality over quantity' as an excuse to keep up hectic lifestyles with infrequent rest, justifying it by making sure that our activities are epic in the small windows of time we have in our hectic lives.

What are the ways you buy back time for and with those you love? Do you do it every day? We will always try to sit down and have our evening meal together as a family. Throughout the day this is one of the things that it is always good to come home for, to take a pause in the day to simply be together and eat together.

What about the time you spend together during the week? Is it time always busying about from one job to the next, replacing employed work with work of another kind, or is it time to be together, delighting in each other?

What about monthly or annual activities? Bex is incredible at booking fun weekend activities and planning lovely holidays, spreading them throughout the year so that we can enjoy space and time together, resting and enjoying God's life as a family.

Rest is a gift! It is a gift that has been given to you, and it is one that you have been encouraged and commanded to embrace. How you do that is up to you, and it's important to find something that fits. Learning to care for yourself is something the world around struggles to embrace. It takes vulnerability, courage and strength to do it, but the benefits of it, especially when it is incorporated into a pattern and rhythm of being, will enrich your life in unexpected and glorious ways. As O'Rourke says: 'Resting is the starting point for our journey to our hearts, but it is only the start. We shall find a new way of seeing and then a new way of loving. Of loving ourselves, and others, and God.'[20]

10

Rest Gets to Work

The God of Genesis is not simply the God who works, but the God who rests as well.

Having spent time reflecting on the biblical and theological rooting of God's gift of rest, and having seen both the strains we face through a lack of it and how we might begin to care for ourselves, I want to move in this chapter to look at how all that ties in with an understanding of work. I hope that I have not given you the impression that work is not a good thing. However, the balance between work and rest has become so skewed, with the pendulum having swung so far away from a healthy understanding of rest, that I have felt the need to address the issue in a spirit of hoping the pendulum can swing back.

Part of that movement of addressing the imbalance comes through highlighting the importance of rest, but movement can also come in understanding a healthy view of work. These two are not the opposites that we often make them out to be, and in this chapter my hope is that we can explore some familiar ground, and in doing so heal that division in our thinking.

I want to begin, where we began earlier . . .

In the Beginning

> In the beginning when God created the heavens and the earth, the earth was a formless void and darkness covered the face of the deep, while a wind from God swept over the face of the waters.[1]

Right here at the beginning of Scripture we see God at work. However, it is important for us to explore what that means, for as with so many passages in Scripture, it is easy for us to jump to the conclusion we want to come to, which may be the wrong one. So right here at the beginning of the chapter I want to set out something for us to hold as we journey through this subject; God does not work like we work. That might sound like an obvious thing to say, but so often our actions betray our theology.

The word we translate as 'created' in Genesis 1:1 is the Hebrew word '*bara*', which is used forty-eight times in the Old Testament. There are a couple of features of that word that are worth focusing on.

Firstly, in all of those forty-eight instances, the subject of the word is always God. This is perhaps one of the main things that stuck with me from my year of Hebrew at Bible college. This is activity that God does that we do not do. Or in other words, God does not work like we work.

This idea of creating is rooted in the idea of creating something out of nothing. In God there was the potential for the other before anything was, but originally, other than God there was nothing. Then there was the stirring of the Spirit over the face of the waters. Translations will vary on whether to use 'wind' or 'Spirit' or 'breath', and all are a perfectly good translation of the word that is used here in Genesis, but the important thing to take from it is that this is God at work. God is doing something here, bringing heaven and earth into being and giving them a sense of order and structure. Then God speaks and there is light. He is the grand designer who is uniquely able to bring about the creation he has imagined.[2]

What we can also see when we look at God at work in creation is his creativity. The cosmos is not a divine self-assembly kit that God quickly knocked together, it is brimming with his creative beauty. As John Goldingay and Robert Innes say in their book *God at Work*: 'God creates, works, with a combination of purpose and playfulness, spontaneity and system.'[3]

God's creativity is expressed through the powerful and yet gentle hovering of his Spirit over the waters, through his spoken word, through his artistry and design and imagination. Fr Richard Rohr puts it like this: 'God clearly loves variety. Just when you think you cannot imagine another shape, type, or way of being in this world, you watch the Nature Channel – or even step outside! – and there is something in the sea, air or earth that you could never have pictured or imagined.'[4]

That heart or spirit of creativity is one that we can reflect as human beings. We are capable of great imagination and creativity, and able to produce beautiful and wondrous things that enhance life. The very first person recorded to be 'filled with the Spirit' was Bezalel in Exodus 31:

The LORD spoke to Moses: See, I have called by name Bezalel son of Uri son of Hur, of the tribe of Judah: and I have filled him with divine spirit, with ability, intelligence, and knowledge in every kind of craft, to devise artistic designs, to work in gold, silver, and bronze, in cutting stones for setting, and in carving wood, in every kind of craft.[5]

It is significant that the God of such wondrous creativity and work should fill with his Spirit one who also shares that creative heart. Bezalel, however, did not create the stones he cut, or the wood he carved, or the gems he set. He simply used his God-given creativity, artistry and skill to forge them into something else. God is the only one who can take nothing and make something. God does not work like we work. There is something, though, of that divine creative spark and potential in us as human beings which, as we connect with it, can be a means of us reflecting God's work.

Another question that arises from Genesis is around what we often refer to as 'the Fall'.

This is what God says to Adam after he and Eve have eaten from the tree:

> Because you have listened to the voice of your wife, and have eaten of the tree about which I commanded you, 'You shall not eat of it,' cursed is the ground because of you; in toil you shall eat of it all the days of your life; thorns and thistles it shall bring forth for you; and you shall eat the plants of the field. By the sweat of your face you shall eat bread until you return to the ground, for out of it you were taken; you are dust, and to dust you shall return.[6]

Is work a curse? According to Graham Dow: 'the pattern of the fall . . . indicates that work becomes simply a sweat to stay alive.'[7]

How you answer that question may well depend on what you do for a living. If you have had an experience of work that has been negative, or destructive, or painful then you may well want to affirm the belief that work is a curse. What about those who enjoy their work? If you go to work and it is a pleasurable experience that gives meaning to your life even when it is hard, you may want to argue that work is not a curse. Are we simply left to answer this question subjectively, or can we be a little bit more objective?

God is a God who works. In saying that, we are using a human word to describe something far bigger than our words could ever convey or our minds understand. We struggle to understand how we can relate to work, let alone what it means for God to work. Genesis does affirm, however, that God works. What the Fall does is bring in a disconnection between us and God. It is wide-reaching; we not only have life but now we have death, we not only have bliss but now we have toil, we not only have relationship but now we have blame. Work is not the curse. The privilege and joy of developing the world under God, and as those in God's image, does not get eradicated at the Fall. It is more that life is now lived in tension between the two. Life is not now simply joy of divine-human co-development, but is now one that is hardened by the need for constant struggle. Work is now not simply defined in our relationship with God, creation and each other, but in independence of that, which brings with it the curse. When we step out of divine relationship, when we step out of creative rhythm, when we step out of personal co-operation, work becomes a curse.

The God of Genesis is not simply the God who works, but the God who rests as well. Life is punctuated with activity and stillness, with work and rest, with purpose and playfulness. 'The pattern of God's story says something to us as workers, and says something to us as people who influence patterns of work for other people.'[8]

Even now we are called to join with God in his work. Even the Fall does not stop God from reaching out and drawing us into himself. Part of the problem with our lack of care for creation is that we think: 'Well, we've already messed it up.' We are given that call every day, each morning anew, to join with God in his work for bringing about peace and harmony to all creation. Work and rest, then, are balanced within that goal. When we work, we are joining with divine activity for the glory of God. When we rest, we are saying that work should look, not just like the image of our culture, but as that which God has gifted. When we rest, we rest in the glory of God:

> It is an immeasurable gift and blessing for individuals to understand how humankind must shape creation according to the divine will and to participate in that divine project. Furthermore, tragedies associated with the world of work can be cured and future dangers avoided if human beings individually and collectively understand their purpose and privilege as co-operative instruments of God's creative power; that they are invited to join with God in a kind of co-creative role.[9]

Commandment to Rest is Also a Commandment to Work

Let's remind ourselves of the Sabbath commandment in Exodus 20:

> Remember the Sabbath day, and keep it holy. Six days you shall labor and do all your work. But the seventh day is a sabbath to the LORD your God; you shall not do any work – you, your son or your daughter, your male or female slave, your livestock, or the alien resident in your towns. For in six days the LORD made

heaven and earth, the sea, and all that is in them, but rested the seventh day; therefore the LORD blessed the sabbath day and consecrated it.[10]

We have already spent a great deal of time exploring how God's people have received and lived the Sabbath, but what is interesting is that relationship *between* work and Sabbath, which is something we often miss in this commandment. If we look at the commandment closely, we see that it says as much about work as it does about rest. It speaks of human work, and it speaks of God's work in creation.

There are as many different interpretations of what work means from this command as there are on what Sabbath means, but I think that if we are to give a wide interpretation to the expression of Sabbath, then we should also do so for our understanding of work.

Firstly, I do not think that we should settle for a definition of work as merely 'employment'. I think one of the great struggles we have put upon ourselves in recent centuries when it comes to a healthy view of work has come from this understanding. It is, I think, a one-dimensional understanding of something that God has given to us, and through which we seek to live in his image. We have confused employment or the goal of making money with the work that God has given, and somehow we have lauded this as a great Christian virtue.

I read an article recently which said that life with no work has no meaning for a Christian. I do not agree with this statement, but there would be some who certainly would, which is why it is so important to think carefully about work as given by God rather that what human beings have allowed it to become defined as. What about those who are not employed for various reasons? Are we really saying that their lives are meaningless?

Are we saying that if they do experience a lack of meaning that a tax form is going to fulfil that?

I recently had coffee with a rabbi in Bristol, which gave me the opportunity to speak with him about his Jewish faith and his understanding of Sabbath. It was a thoroughly enjoyable time which gave me a great deal more insight into a Jewish understanding of Sabbath than I had gleaned from the running dialogue between Jesus and the Pharisees in the gospels. What my new friend talked about was how the commandment gives them a double blessing, to be active and to rest. For him this activity (or work) is a blessing given by God that we are commanded to embrace. It is, however, as the commandment makes clear to us, something we do in response to the activity (or work) of God.

God's work is not simply about employment. He does not get paid, he has no boss, he is part of no trade union, he is not paying into a pension scheme. He does not even pay tax!

'In societies influenced by western values and ways of working, the temptation is immense to try to create ourselves and justify our existence through our work.'[11] When it comes to work, so much of how we define ourselves is taken from what we do. Now don't get me wrong, I'm not against making money or having wealth, but these days so many people try to find themselves through an endless exploration of work, moving from one thing to another in search of what already lies within them. We keep on working because we believe that in doing so we will eventually come to the pot of gold at the end of the rainbow, a version of ourselves that we can live with, where we are content, fulfilled and at peace. God does not work like we work.

What we see with God's work is a creative expression born out of who he is, which flows out for the good of the other.

I believe that this is the work that is truly blessed by God, which we are commanded to embrace in all its glorious diversity

and colour. This comes out of the expression of who you have
been created to be. Not who your parents say you should be, or
what society dictates you should be, or what your career adviser
advised you should be; but who God has created *you* to be.
That unique spirit, that creative force, that part of you that is
awakened through experiencing the life of God flowing in and
through you. When we operate from this place, when we seek
to engage and connect with the world around us for good, for
its good, as those expressing something deep within the nature
and character of God, then this is holy work. It is the holy
work of a mother or father taking time out of employment to
raise children. It is the holy work of the volunteer. It is the holy
work of the employed who work from this place. It is the holy
longing of those who long for this to be their reality, but who
for various reasons cannot, but whose hearts still beat with the
same beat of their Creator.

It is about connection. Connection with God, with ourselves, with the people and world around us. It is this connection that we are in danger of losing as we continue deeper
into a world that is defining work as simply the mindless and
tyrannical pursuit of personal wealth and ambition.

Catherine McGeachy points out that we are 'trying to fit many
essential and meaningful tasks into a diminishing window of
time and, in doing so, have found that some tasks have become
casualties. The result? People have become disconnected from
their traditional spiritual, family and social communities'.[12]

In a recent BBC Radio 4 interview[13] with his son Harry,
Prince Charles talked about environmental issues and how as
human beings we have lost our proper connection with the
natural world.

I agree with him, as do an increasing number of people who
know that we desperately need to rediscover these connections.

Perhaps, then, rest is the place where this rediscovery can begin, for it is in this place that we are infused once more with the life of God, and can then begin to work from a place of rest.

My Father is Still Working

In John chapter 5 we see an account of Jesus healing on the Sabbath. He heals a lame man who does not initially know who has healed him, but later comes and discovers that it is Jesus. We pick up that story in verse 15:

> The man went away and told the Jews that it was Jesus who had made him well. Therefore the Jews started persecuting Jesus, because he was doing such things on the sabbath. But Jesus answered them, 'My Father is still working, and I also am working.' For this reason the Jews were seeking all the more to kill him, because he was not only breaking the sabbath, but was also calling God his own Father, thereby making himself equal to God.[14]

Some translations have given us 'My Father is always working'.[15] However, I think it is important when we look at the gospels to look at what we have learned so far from the revelation of God's Spirit speaking through Scripture, and the context in which the Spirit speaks in this particular moment.

Think back to what we have seen already about God's rest in Genesis. Should we say that God is always working? In order to do that we have to think about the discussion we have just come from about our work.

Is 'always' a measurement of time or consistency? If it is a measurement of time, then what we are saying is that God does not stop working, which seems to fly in the face of what we see in the creation accounts, and what God confirms time and time again to his people about his stopping work to rest on the seventh day.

If it is a measurement of consistency, then what we are saying is that the work that God has done is the same work Jesus refers to, and is the same work that God continues to do to this day. This seems to me to be a much more faithful response to the wider counsel of Scripture. If God's work is a creative expression that is born out of who he is, which flows out for the good of the other, then we can rightly say that God is still at work, always at work, because this is who God eternally is. This helps us to understand what we could mean by 'always'. It should not be used to essentially say, 'God isn't taking a break, why should I/you?' My answer to that question is two-fold. Firstly, I am not God; God does not work like we work. Secondly, it is a clear biblical truth, raised again and again that God did take a break to rest, and that he commands those he has called to do the same. To not take a break, to fail to rest in your work, even when that work is in keeping with the creative self-expression of pouring out to the other, would be, as Ian Stackhouse cautions, 'vaunting oneself above God'.[16]

Here, though, Jesus heals the man who was lame. On the Sabbath. So perhaps here there is a tying in of rest and work again, which we have been exploring in this chapter. This is not some random good work, or an orchestrated act of religious defiance. It is far more organic than that. Jesus healed this man because this is what God has been doing from the beginning, because this is who God is. And what the Father does, the Son does; that's what Jesus goes on to say later in chapter 5: 'Very truly, I tell you, the Son can do nothing on his own, but only what he sees the Father doing; for whatever the Father does, the Son does likewise.'[17]

This is part of the eternal nature of God, the one whose creative expression is born out of who he is; which flows out for the good of the other; the one who offers us life then can infuse us in the deep places, bringing true rest and healing to the places where we need it most. That is his work, which we have already seen in Colossians 1: 'So spacious is he, so roomy, that everything of God finds its proper place in him without crowding. Not only that, but all the broken and dislocated pieces of the universe – people and things, animals and atoms – get properly fixed and fit together in vibrant harmonies, all because of his death, his blood that poured down from the cross.'[18]

In these Sabbath healings we see the coming together of work and rest. Sabbath is not merely an end in itself, where our lack of activity is the sole benefit. It is not simply about ticking the boxes to say that you have done certain things or not done other things. That's when Sabbath becomes legalistic. That's the danger Tony Horsfall warns us of, that we are 'led back into legalism and the kind of bondage that lays down rules and regulations about what we should or should not do'.[19] There is a bigger picture to Sabbath rest, as there so often is with the things of God. What sets it apart from the legalism of the religious leaders of Jesus' day, and the legalism of our own, is the 'so that'; that I do not merely choose this or abstain from that because I should, but *so that* I might enter more deeply into the life of God. Jesus did not heal this man because he wanted to break the Sabbath law, or because in his interpretation healing him was keeping it, but *so that* this man might experience the life that God has freely brought through Christ.

This work is important. If this is the work we can bring to our employment, then it will enrich it. If this is the work that we can bring to raising our families, they will be enriched. If this is the life you hope for but do not yet experience, then it will break into your life in unexpected rays of grace. This is where the two meet, in the place where God's wondrous creativity is born in us again and again, where his life infuses every area of our own. We are not burdened with a more palatable or achievable or Christianity-centred set of obligations and rules, but are truly set free to experience life in all its fullness.

Horsfall says: 'Once secured, this place becomes the springboard for our activity, which flows naturally out of our connectedness with God.'[20]

This life bursts through into all we do, like the light that bursts through a stained-glass window and colours all inside with its beauty, and gives us the freedom to live as those created in the image of God, to do the work that his children are called to do, in whatever way that looks like to you.

11

As It Was in the Beginning

It is because God loves you that he gives you the gift of rest, not so that you might be someone else, but so that you might be more fully and more truly you.

As we come to the end of this journey, I find myself hopeful. The very fact that you are reading these words means that you are still on that journey, and have no doubt, you will continue long after this book is gathering dust on the shelf. I am hopeful, not because of what is in this book, but because of what God might have stirred in you through this journey.

I am often struck by how much of what has genuine worth flies in the face of the prevailing culture of our time, and how foolish it seems. One example I have already mentioned illustrates this well for me. When I came to the church here in Bath, I told the leadership of my intention to take a five-day week rather than a six-day week, because I would get more done in five days than in six. On the face of it, this seems foolish. With a whole other day, think of all that could be accomplished, think of all the extra good that could be done; why give up that day? That would have been my thinking some time ago, but not now, because I have learned (and am still learning) through my own struggle and failings, the wisdom of foolishness: that sometimes, in order to recover your life, you need to give up the day. Or rather, set apart the day not simply as a means of recovery or refuelling, but as a holy offering, and as space in which to be infused with the life of God. Whatever the culture of my time is telling me, I have learned that there is wisdom in that.

The Wisdom of Rest

When we journey through the Bible, we come across the figure of wisdom, and the more we study wisdom, the more we become aware that she is far more beautiful, and much more different than we ever imagined. The way we view the world, and tend to view wisdom in the world, is that it is something to acquire, something to possess. If I learn the right pieces of knowledge and I acquire the right bits of information from the right people so that I can get ahead in life, then I am wise; then I possess wisdom. Yet we all know knowledgeable people who are far from wise, and those who aren't learned who are very wise.

When we look at the Wisdom tradition of the Bible, we come across these words in Proverbs:

> Happy are those who find wisdom,
> and those who get understanding,
> for her income is better than silver,
> and her revenue better than gold.
> She is more precious than jewels,

and nothing you desire can compare with her.
Long life is in her right hand;
in her left hand are riches and honor.
Her ways are ways of pleasantness,
and all her paths are peace.
She is a tree of life to those who lay hold of her;
those who hold her fast are called happy.[1]

Wisdom is not a possession but a person, or rather, that is how the wisdom writers expressed her. You have to know her, to be connected to her, to listen to her, to seek her because when you approach wisdom like that, as a suitor rather than a collector, then it is impossible to measure the worth.

We need to know wisdom in rest. For me, this whole journey has not been about acquiring a bunch of facts which will make me more learned about my need to rest. I know I need to rest, my soul longs for the deep rest we have been exploring, and I am sure that the same is true for many of you. So in closing this book I know that what I need is to court the wisdom of rest. To know her, to be connected to her, to listen to her and to seek her. To hear her voice calling in the midst of the hustle and bustle. That's the image that the writer of Proverbs begins with:

Wisdom cries out in the street;
in the squares she raises her voice.
At the busiest corner she cries out . . .[2]

We do not hear wisdom's call in the busy squares, marketplaces, office blocks, family homes, universities and bustling street corners because this is where wisdom can be found, but because this is where wisdom is needed, where wisdom needs to be known.

Rest, as we have been exploring it, is rooted within this Wisdom tradition because it connects us to a deeper sense of life. It refuses to let us be satisfied with simply knowing about good practice, and takes us deeper to experience the life that can only come with connectedness to our humanity, to the rest of creation, and to the Creator. When we find that connection, we root ourselves in the deepest truths of the cosmos, the truths that are about who we are rather than simply what we do. In some ways our age is guilty of the paradox that we have simplified, or at times oversimplified things, but in doing so have made them more complicated. Let me put it like this: when we simplify everything down to I am what I do, then rest just becomes another thing that I have to do, but viewing rest that way actually complicates our lives because we didn't have enough time to 'get things done' to begin with. So wisdom cries out to the writer of Proverbs generation, and to ours:

'How long, O simple ones, will you love being simple?'[3]

Rather than being simple, we are talking about deep things here, things not simply to be known, but to be connected with.

I remember when our son, Leo, was just over a year old his sleep routine was disturbed as the clocks went back. So for almost six months we were up at 4 a.m. each day, having only managed to get him down at perhaps 10 p.m. the night before. So when I started work in the morning, I had already been up five hours. I well remember one time being so tired that I couldn't button my shirt, and had to sleep. I had reached the end of myself and simply could not carry on. How many of us have reached the end of ourselves more times than we would care to recall? I can think of other times in my life when I have been forced to rest, whether it has been through personal tragedy or sheer exhaustion, and I am sure many of you will know those times all too well. These are moments in some ways beyond our control. I could not keep my son asleep through sheer willpower, even if I had wanted to. There are some things that we just cannot push. Can we develop though, a consciousness and connectedness deep within us that allows us to experience life even at the end of ourselves, to hear the voice of wisdom calling in the loud busy streets of our lives, to experience and be infused with the very life of God, even when it feels as though the cup, far from overflowing, has run dry?

These are the things we have been exploring, and my plea to you would be to keep exploring them. Several years ago I felt challenged to seek a greater humility in my life, and so I did what I think many people would do in that situation, I bought a book. It came highly recommended, seemed to deal with some of the areas I was hoping it would from the reviews, and so I excitedly began to read. No sooner had I got to the introduction, than the writer was essentially saying, 'If you want to learn humility you can't read it in a book!' You can imagine my disappointment as a consumer having already parted with my £7.99, being left with the feeling that they really should have put that information on the back. It actually turned out to be a very good book.

Part of the problem I have already highlighted is that we approach this like consumers. We have a need, we want to purchase something to alleviate that need, and we expect value for money.

You have bought this book, which I trust was value for money (although I do not set the price), and I hope it has met you in a place of need. However, we cannot learn to rest by reading a book. There comes a time when there are no more pages to turn and we are left in the day-to-day reality of the world, with all its challenges and delights.

It might be that you have struggled to find the balance and rhythm of rest in your life, and perhaps this has made you feel foolish in a culture that prides itself on its own brand of work ethic. In the book of Proverbs, one of the characters who comes up again and again is the 'fool'. The fool is the one who despises wisdom, who will not hear her call, the one who isn't hungry and thirsty for that which is deeper. The fool is the one who essentially rejects being infused with God's life.

If you have been self-aware enough to look into your life and know that the balance is wrong; if you have become dissatisfied with viewing rest simply as recovery; if you are hungry for a deeper connection with yourself, with others and with God; and if you are thirsty for an infusion of his life in your own, you are anything but foolish! You are taking those steps of pilgrimage that we spoke about earlier, and according to the psalmist there is blessing in that:

'Blessed are those whose strength is in you, whose hearts are set on pilgrimage.'[4]

Putting Boundaries in Place

'Boundary' is a word that raises mixed emotions. On the one hand it seems a bit restrictive, almost exclusive, which stems I think from our natural tendency as human beings to try to keep out that which we do not want. Many of us know what it is like to be on the other side of the boundary, to be excluded and to feel unwanted, so perhaps we have a natural dislike for boundaries. Or we have recognized the need for boundaries, in our work, home, family, social lives, but have struggled to put them in place. Perhaps we have failed. We say things like, 'I find boundaries hard.'

Rather than saying that we need to try harder, perhaps it is our thinking that needs to shift.

Boundaries are a part of everyday life, we move through them and cross over them and are held within them every single day. We drive down the motorway, trusting that the cars coming in the other direction cannot veer over to our carriageway and cause us fatal harm. We close the doors to our homes at night, locking them, shutting the windows and trusting that this will keep us safe. We open the seal on food products we buy, trusting that it has remained intact and the food we have bought has not spoiled.

Our whole life is a journey between boundary time. Monday will become Tuesday, which will become Wednesday etc. We do not usually lay awake at night fearful that we will lose a day, that all of a sudden Thursday will simply vanish. The sun rises and the sun sets each day. We do not drift aimlessly into the darkness of space, but are held in our orbit around the sun. We trust these boundaries every single day, most of the time without even thinking. So why is it that we struggle so much with putting boundaries into our own lives?

Perhaps we do not trust them as we do these other boundaries? Perhaps we are uncertain that they will be for our good in a culture that bombards us with its own alternatives. Maybe the idea of Sabbath and rest seem to be so subversive in our culture that they just get drowned out.

Whatever pressures exist in life, however many demands there are, you alone are the master of how you spend your time. Nobody is standing behind you with a gun to your head. This is not meant to be critical or to make you feel a sense of failure; quite the opposite. I have found it very liberating to know that I ultimately have control over what I spend my time on. I can put those boundaries in place, if I trust that they will do me good, if I trust that they are worth the time and effort to be built.

Perhaps the time has come to think, or think again, about what it is that we want from life. Do we trust those words of

Jesus: 'I came so they can have real and eternal life, more and better life than they ever dreamed of'?[5]

What does that life look like for you? For your family? Are you hungry and thirsty for more of it? How much are you willing to lay down for it?

Start to set that time aside. Little by little, moment by moment, but be intentional about it and protective of it. Dorothy Bass said, 'without time, no bandage will be on the wound, no supper on the table, no roof on the building. Time in itself is not enough, but when time is absent, nothing else is present.'[6]

Unless we set aside the time, unless we put in the boundaries, then we will find ourselves slipping back into old habits, veering across the carriageway or drifting off into the endless void of stolen time.

If what you need to do is to start small, then start small. If what you need to do is the big gesture, then make it big. My advice would be to make it realistic. If you struggle, one hour a day may not be currently within your grasp. Thirty minutes, though, may be very possible, and if you take thirty minutes on a regular basis within your week to be open to the life of God through rest, then that will make a big difference to your life as a whole. More often than not, you will also find it a springboard to more time.

Shelly Miller encourages us:

Take a long prayer walk alone with the dog, linger long in pyjamas while savouring a cup of tea and journal random thoughts. Baby steps. You work two jobs and fall asleep when you finally sit down? Take your lunch hour in a peaceful spot alone, once or a few times a week. Listen, write down what you hear, and practice adoration. You may not have time for a whole day to rest, but a small window of time here and there cultivates a Sabbath heart.'[7]

New Every Morning

I want to end by reflecting on something we have already explored, but which is well worth highlighting. You are valued and loved *as you are*! The gift of rest that is given to you through God's example in creation, through Sabbath, through Jesus, is not designed to highlight your inadequacies. It is not designed to make you feel 'great, here is another thing I'm meant to do but can't'. It is because God loves you that he gives you the gift of rest, not so that you might be someone else, but so that you might be more fully and more truly you. He gives that rest to me in love, so that I might be the best husband, father, friend, colleague, pastor and human being I can, and to find the space that those things might find their proper connection.

It is when I find that rest which infuses me with his life that I am truly held in who I am before him. Not what I do, or have been, or hope to be, but who I am in this moment. Yet who I am in this moment is also bound up in the truth of the one who says: 'I am making all things new.'[8] It is bound up in the truth of the writer of Lamentations who says:

> The steadfast love of the LORD never ceases,
> his mercies never come to an end;
> they are new every morning;
> great is your faithfulness.[9]

In his book *The Day is Yours,* Ian Stackhouse reflects on this verse: 'In that sense, as Augustine mused in De Genesi as Litteram, we are always in day one of creation.'[10]

Rather than feeling as though we are trapped in an endless Groundhog Day of creation, Ian explores the liberation that can come through this thinking: 'To live in day one is to wake up with the knowledge that this new day is infused with that same Genesis light that exploded onto the world by divine fiat.'[11]

As we take the time to rest we are bathed in the light of who we are as God's children, but are also found within the eternal stream of God's life that flows ever towards the ocean of eternity. An eternity that is not measured in length of years, but in its depth of meaning. Given that this is the river we drift along in, how much of our time is orientated around what we have to do, around how much time we have left or around how much time is running through the hourglass? Dorothy Bass reflected on time: 'All of us wonder, naturally, about the quantity of this measure. More important, however, is its quality.'[12]

What is the quality of your life? Or is it focused solely on 'how much time'? Rest sets us free from thinking that everything needs to be measured, or driven, or managed. It allows us to simply be; be in the world, be with each other, be part of the cosmos and be connected to the Divine. Can such things be measured? Should they? Or rather, are we made new every morning, as those first rays of light and life infused a formless and empty world?

I know that life is busy. I know there are endless calls on our time, commitments that have to be honoured, tasks that need to be done. This is the reality of life in the twenty-first century, and to some extent, life has always been like this. This is not the only truth, though, nor even the most important one.

We are constantly seeking to define the Divine, to understand ourselves within his light and to understand how then we are called to live. Our language fails us every time, and so God spoke his own word in the giving of his Son. And the words he spoke were truth on a deeper level than we could ever hope to understand, truth that gets down to the bones of us, the cells that make us up – that you are created in love and are treasured by the one who created you; that far from your mistakes being the things that define you, you are met with endless, boundless grace and patience; that the goal of your life is not to be a better Christian, or to read the Bible more, or to pray more, although all those things are good. The goal for your life is to be like Jesus; to be transformed little by little, through the chrysalis of the Spirit, into the image and likeness of the one who says he is life itself in all its vibrancy and colour. Paul puts it like this when he writes to Christians in Rome in the first century: 'God knew what he was doing from the very beginning. He decided from the outset to shape the lives of those who love him along the same lines as the life of his Son.'[13]

So your life and mine are slowly and softly being shaped along the same lines as Christ's.

God's desire for you is not to be bound up in religion, to be set free from one chain only to tie yourself up with another. His desire for you is freedom, is life that is full and lasting and nourishes you deep within. It is life that will truly give you rest as it infuses every part of you. It is life that will enrich your waking and sleeping, your working and resting, your coming and going. It is a rest that he delights in, that he brought into being, and he longs for it to be a delight for you too.

From the source of all things, from the beginning, this has always been true. It is the whisper of the Spirit hovering over the waters, it is the fingerprint of creation rustling through the trees, it is the voice of wisdom calling in the marketplace. When we connect with these things, we root ourselves in the deepest truths of the cosmos. We find life! Life in the one who is the wisdom of God, who calls throughout the ages to tired and weary ones:

Come to me . . . and I will give you rest.[14]

Notes

Introduction

[1] Isaiah 30:15.

1 A Challenging Journey

[1] Felicity Callard, Kimberley Staines, James Wilkes, eds. *The Restless Compendium* (Cham: Springer International Publishing, 2016), pp. 59–67.

[2] Callard, Staines, Wilkes, eds. *The Restless Compendium*, p. 64.

[3] Luke 5:17–26.

[4] David Murray, *Reset: Living a Grace-Paced Life in a Burnout Culture* (Wheaton, IL: Crossway, 2017), p. 24.

[5] John 10:10.

[6] Mark Buchanan, *The Rest of God* (Nashville, TN: Thomas Nelson, 2006), p. 1.

2 In the Beginning

[1] Genesis 1:1.

[2] Habakkuk 1:12a, NIV 2011.

[3] Augustine, *Confessions 11.13.15.*

4   For further discussion see Angela Tilby, *Let There Be Light: Praying with Genesis* (London: Darton, Longman & Todd, 2006), p. 18.

5   J. Philip Newell, *The Book of Creation: The Practice of Celtic Spirituality* (Norwich: Canterbury Press, 1999), p. 101.

6   Genesis 1:3–5.

7   Genesis 1:11.

8   Genesis 1:14–16.

9   John Davies, *God at Work: Creation Then and Now – A Practical Exploration* (Norwich: Canterbury Press, 2001), p. 8.

10 See Tilby, *Let There Be Light*, p. 39.

11 Ecclesiastes 3:1–8.

12 Mandy Barrow, 'The Reason for the Seasons', *Primary Homework Help* (2013), http://www.primaryhomeworkhelp.co.uk/time/seasons.htm (accessed 18 April 2018).

13 See Emmanuel Mignot, 'Why we sleep', *PLOS Biology* (2008) http://journals.plos.org/plosbiology/article?id=10.1371/journal.pbio.0060106 (accessed 18 April 2018).

14 Brooke Borel, 'Do Plants Sleep?' *Popular Science* (2014) https://www.popsci.com/blog-network/our-modern-plagues/do-plants-sleep (accessed 27 July 2017).

15 Genesis 1:5,8,13,19,23,31.

16 Newell, *The Book of Creation*, p. 104.

17 2 Corinthians 3:17.

18 *All Things Bright and Beautiful*, words by Cecil Frances Alexander, 1818–1895.

19 Genesis 1:28.

20 See discussion in Douglas J. Moo, 'Creation and New Creation: Transforming Christian Perspectives' in *Creation in Crisis: Christian Perspectives on Sustainability* (ed. Robert S. White; London: SPCK, 2009), pp. 252–4.

21 Genesis 2:15, NIV 2011.

22 Genesis 1:27.

23 See discussion in Norman Wirzba, *From Nature to Creation: A Christian Vision for Understanding and Loving Our World* (Grand Rapids, MI: Baker Academic, 2015), pp. 6–7.

24 Shelly Miller, *Rhythms of Rest: Finding the Spirit of Sabbath in a Busy World* (Minneapolis, MN: Bethany House, 2016), p. 15.

3 The God Who Rests

1   Genesis 2:1–3.
2   Isaiah 40:28.
3   John H. Walton, *Genesis,* The NIV Application Commentary (Grand Rapids, MI: Zondervan, 2001), p. 148.
4   1 John 4:8.
5   1 John 3:1.
6   Genesis 1:4,10,12,18,21,25.
7   Genesis 1:31.
8   Psalm 104:31.
9   Newell, *The Book of Creation*, p. 103.
10 Tilby, *Let There Be Light*, p. 111.
11 Explored in the work of Max Weber, late nineteenth/early twentieth-century German sociologist.
12 James 2:26b.
13 Davies, *God at Work*, p. 52.
14 Genesis 2:3a, NIV 2011.
15 Genesis 1:22.
16 Genesis 1:28.
17 Genesis 2:3.
18 Genesis 1:4,10,12,18,21,25,31.
19 Jürgen Moltmann, *God in Creation: An Ecological Doctrine of Creation* (London: SCM Press Ltd., 1985), p. 278.
20 Tilby, *Let There Be Light*, p. 111.
21 See discussion in Gordon I. Wenham, *Genesis 1–15*, Word Biblical Commentary series (Nashville, TN: Thomas Nelson, 1987), p. 35.
22 Robert Alter, *The Five Books of Moses: A Translation with Commentary* (London: W.W. Norton & Company, 2004), p. 20.

4 Receiving Sabbath

1   John 14:6.
2   Matthew 5:17.
3   Abraham Joshua Heschel, *The Sabbath* (New York: Farrar, Straus and Giroux, 1951), p. 17.

4   Exodus 20:8–11.
5   For helpful discussion see Terence E. Fretheim, *Exodus*, Interpretation commentary series (Louisville, KY: Westminster John Knox Press, 1991), p. 229 and Peter Enns, *Exodus*, The NIV Application Commentary (Grand Rapids, MI: Zondervan, 2000), p. 418.
6   Exodus 2:24, emphasis mine.
7   Exodus 16:23.
8   See Gordon MacDonald, *Ordering Your Private World* (Nashville, TN: Thomas Nelson, 2012).
9   The foundational work in the literature of Jewish mystical thought.
10 Exodus 20:10.
11 See discussion in Dayan Grunfeld, *The Sabbath: A Guide to its Understanding and Observance* (Jerusalem: Feldheim Publishers, 1981), pp. 65–6.
12 Heschel, *The Sabbath*, pp. 31–2.
13 See discussion in Grunfeld, *The Sabbath*, pp. 23–37.
14 Psalm 46:10.
15 See Robert Alter, *The Book of Psalms: A Translation with Commentary* (London: W.W. Norton & Company, 2007), p. 165.
16 Heschel, *The Sabbath*, p. 13.
17 Acts 17:28.
18 Exodus 20:11.
19 Psalm 118:24.
20 Leviticus 11:44,45; 19:2; 20:7.
21 Patrick D. Miller, *The Ten Commandments*, Interpretation commentary series (Louisville, KY: Westminster John Knox Press, 2009), p. 125.
22 Deuteronomy 5:12–14.
23 Deuteronomy 5:15.
24 Heschel, *The Sabbath*, p. 14.

5 Living Sabbath

1   See https://www.chabad.org/library/article_cdo/aid/253215/jewish/Shabbat.htm (accessed 10 May 2018).

2   Colossians 2:16,17.
3   Isaiah 12:3.
4   Romans 12:1,2.
5   Marva J. Dawn, *Keeping the Sabbath Wholly: Ceasing, Resting, Embracing, Feasting* (Grand Rapids, MI: Eerdmans, 1989), p. x.
6   Norman Wirzba, *Living the Sabbath: Discovering the Rhythms of Rest and Delight* (Grand Rapids, MI: Brazos Press, 2006), p. 154.
7   Romans 12:1, *The Message*.
8   Song of Solomon 6:3.
9   John 13:34.
10 Dan B. Allender, *Sabbath* (Nashville, TN: Thomas Nelson, 2009), p. 68.
11 Psalm 34:8.
12 Allender, *Sabbath*, p. 65.
13 J.John, *Ten: Living the Ten Commandments in the 21st Century* (Eastbourne: Kingsway Communications Ltd., 2000), p. 209.
14 Wirzba, *Living the Sabbath*, p. 115.
15 Isaiah 56:6,7.
16 Walter Brueggemann, *Sabbath as Resistance: Saying No to the Culture of Now* (Louisville, KY: Westminster John Knox Press, 2014), p. 54.
17 J.John, *Ten*, p. 209.
18 Deuteronomy 30:19, NIV 2011.
19 Peter Brain, *Going the Distance: How to Stay Fit for a Lifetime of Ministry* (Kingsford: Matthias Media, 2006), p. 46.
20 Wirzba, *Living the Sabbath*, p. 110.

6 Lord of the Sabbath

1   Tom Wright, *Simply Jesus: Who He Was, What He Did, Why It Matters* (London: SPCK, 2011), p. 134.
2   Luke 9:23.
3   Acts 7.
4   L'Arche is a worldwide federation of people, with and without learning disabilities, working together for a world where all belong.
5   See discussion in Jean Vanier, *Community and Growth* (London: Darton, Longman & Todd, 2007), pp. 177–81.
6   Vanier, *Community and Growth*, p. 177.

160 *Notes*

7 Matthew 12:1–8.
8 See Donald A. Hagner, *Matthew 1–13*, Word Biblical Commentary (Dallas, TX: Word Books, 1993), p. 261.
9 For fuller discussion see Michael J. Wilkins, *Matthew*, The NIV Application Commentary (Grand Rapids, MI: Zondervan, 2004), pp. 440–41.
10 Tom Wright, *Matthew for Everyone: Part 1* (London: SPCK, 2002), p. 140.
11 Mark 2:27.
12 Tilby, *Let There Be Light*, p. 114.
13 Isaiah 58:13,14.
14 Irving M. Zeitlin, *Jesus and the Judaism of His Time* (Cambridge: Polity Press, 1988), p. 76.
15 Matthew 22:37–40.
16 James D.G. Dunn, *Jesus Remembered: Christianity in the Making* (Grand Rapids, MI: Eerdmans, 2003), p. 565.
17 Matthew 12:8.
18 Colossians 1:18–20, *The Message*.
19 1 Samuel 13:14.
20 John 1:18, *The Message*.
21 Ephesians 3:18,19.
22 Matthew 12:9–14.
23 Géza Vermes, *Jesus in the Jewish World* (London: SCM Press, 2010), p. 20.
24 See Hagner, *Matthew 1–13*, p. 262.
25 Tony Horsfall, *Working from a Place of Rest: Jesus and the Key to Sustaining Ministry* (Abingdon: The Bible Reading Fellowship, 2010), p. 63.
26 John 10:10.

7 Come to Me

1 Matthew 11:28.
2 Commonly attributed to Augustine.
3 Luke 10:38–42.

4   John Nolland, *Luke 9:21 – 18:34*, Word Biblical Commentary (Dallas, TX: Word Books, 1993), p. 142.

5   William Barclay, *The Gospel of Luke* (Edinburgh: Saint Andrew Press, 1975), p. 141.

6   Darrell L. Bock, *Luke*, The NIV Application Commentary (Grand Rapids, MI: Zondervan, 1996), p. 304.

7   Horsfall, *Working from a Place of Rest*, p. 60.

8   John 4:3–6.

9   Horsfall, *Working from a Place of Rest*, p. 56.

10 Mark 6:30–32.

11 Mark 6:12,13.

12 Ephesians 5:14b–16.

13 Horsfall, *Working from a Place of Rest*, p. 59.

14 BBC Radio 2, *The Jeremy Vine Show*, broadcast 5 October 2018.

15 Matthew 11:28–30, *The Message*.

16 Wright, *Matthew for Everyone*, p. 137.

17 Wilkins, *Matthew*, p. 423.

18 Robin R. Meyers, *Saving Jesus from the Church: How to Stop Worshiping Christ and Start Following Jesus* (New York: HarperCollins, 2009), p. 148.

19 Pete Greig, *God on Mute: Engaging the Silence of Unanswered Prayer* (Eastbourne: Kingsway, 2007), p. 16.

20 Original source unknown but see https://www.catholicapostolatecenter. org/blog/something-strange-is-happening (accessed 17 December 2018).

21 Tom Smail, *Once and For All: A Confession of the Cross* (Eugene, OR: Wipf & Stock Publishers, 1998), p. 139.

22 Smail, *Once and For All*, p. 139.

8 Feeling the Strain

1   Rodney Green, *90,000 Hours: Managing the World of Work* (Bletchley: Scripture Union, 2002), p. 68.

2   'Rest and Recreation', article in *Psychologies* magazine, March 2017, p. 62.

3 https://www.npr.org/sections/thetwo-way/2018/05/20/612798691/
bishop-michael-currys-royal-wedding-sermon-full-text-of-the-
power-of-love (accessed 10.1.19).

4 Archibald Hart, *The Hidden Link Between Adrenaline and Stress:
The Exciting New Breakthrough That Helps You Overcome Stress
Damage* (Nashville, TN: W. Publishing Group, 1995), p. 44.

5 http://www.thegardenroom-treatments.co.uk/latestnews/and-
sleep-zzzz/ (accessed 25 June 2018).

6 'Rest and Recreation', article in *Psychologies* magazine, March
2017, p. 58.

7 Hart, *The Hidden Link Between Adrenaline and Stress,* p. 44.

8 Hart, *The Hidden Link Between Adrenaline and Stress,* p. 40.

9 Gaius Davies, *Stress: Sources and Solutions* (Fearn: Christian Focus
Publications, 2005), p. 70.

10 Katherine Darton, *How to Manage Stress* (London: Mind,
2012), p. 9.

11 Darton, *How to Manage Stress,* p. 9.

12 Brain, *Going the Distance,* pp. 28–9.

13 Bob Burns, *Resilient Ministry: What Pastors Told Us About Surviv-
ing and Thriving* (Downers Grove, IL: IVP, 2013), p. 61.

14 Brain, *Going the Distance,* p. 10.

9 You're Worth It

1 1 Corinthians 11:26, *The Message.*

2 Matthew 11:28.

3 Allender, *Sabbath*, p. 82.

4 Ephesians 2:4,5.

5 Mark 12:31.

6 Philippians 2:5–8.

7 Richard Rohr, *Simplicity: The Freedom of Letting Go* (New York:
The Crossroad Publishing Company, 2004), p. 170.

8 Isaiah 40:28–31.

9 https://hbr.org/2015/10/how-1-performance-improvements-led-
to-olympic-gold (accessed 12 June 2018).

10 See https://www.robertjmorgan.com/devotional/dont-kill-the-horse/ (accessed 17 December 2018).

11 Murray, *Rest*, pp. 81–2.

12 Eugene Peterson, *The Contemplative Pastor: Returning to the Art of Spiritual Direction* (Grand Rapids, MI: Eerdmans, 1989), p. 18.

13 Psalm 37:7.

14 Buchanan, *The Rest of God*, p. 130.

15 Benignus O'Rourke OSA, *Finding Your Hidden Treasure: The Way of Silent Prayer* (Liguori: Liguori Publications, 2010), p. 90.

16 Augustine, *Confessions* 5.2.

17 St Patrick's Breastplate, https://www.ourcatholicprayers.com/st-patricks-breastplate.html (accessed 17 December 2018).

18 Margaret Feinberg, *Wonderstruck* (Brentwood, TN: Worthy Publishing, 2012), p. 66.

19 Murray, *Reset*, p. 162.

20 O'Rourke, *Finding Your Hidden Treasure*, p. 63.

10 Rest Gets to Work

1 Genesis 1:1,2.

2 For interesting discussion see Walton, *Genesis*, pp. 70–1.

3 John Goldingay and Robert Innes, *God at Work* (Bramcote: Grove Books Ltd., 1994), p. 4.

4 Richard Rohr, *The Divine Dance* (London: SPCK, 2016), p. 114.

5 Exodus 31:1–5.

6 Genesis 3:17–19.

7 Graham Dow, *A Christian Understanding of Daily Work* (Bramcote: Grove Books Ltd., 1994), p. 6.

8 Goldingay and Innes, *God at Work*, p. 11.

9 John Jukes, ed., *A Spirituality of Work* (London: Catholic Media, 2001), p. 21.

10 Exodus 20:8–11.

11 Darrell Cosden, *The Heavenly Good of Earthly Work* (Milton Keynes: Paternoster, 2006), p. 105.

[12] Catherine McGeachy, *Spiritual Intelligence in the Workplace* (Dublin: Veritas Publications, 2001), pp. 25–6.

[13] The *Today* programme on 27 December 2017, which Prince Harry guest edited.

[14] John 5:15–18.

[15] See GNT and NLT.

[16] Ian Stackhouse, *The Day is Yours* (Milton Keynes: Paternoster, 2014), p. 32.

[17] John 5:19.

[18] Colossians 1:19,20, *The Message*.

[19] Horsfall, *Working from a Place of Rest*, p. 66.

[20] Horsfall, *Working from a Place of Rest*, p. 100.

11 As It Was in the Beginning

[1] Proverbs 3:13–18.

[2] Proverbs 1:20,21a.

[3] Proverbs 1:22a.

[4] Psalm 84:5, NIV 2011.

[5] John 10:10, *The Message*.

[6] Dorothy C. Bass, *Receiving the Day* (Hoboken, NJ: Jossey-Bass, 2001), p. 117.

[7] Miller, *Rhythms of Rest*, p. 36.

[8] Revelation 21:5.

[9] Lamentations 3:22,23.

[10] Stackhouse, *The Day is Yours*, p. 132.

[11] Stackhouse, *The Day is Yours*, p. 132.

[12] Bass, *Receiving the Day*, p. 116.

[13] Romans 8:29, *The Message*.

[14] Matthew 11:28.

Bibliography

Allender, D.B., *Sabbath* (Nashville, TN: Thomas Nelson, 2009).

Alter, R., *The Book of Psalms: A Translation with Commentary* (London: W.W. Norton & Company, 2007).

Alter, R., *The Five Books of Moses: A Translation with Commentary* (London: W.W. Norton & Company, 2004).

Augustine, *Confessions*.

Barclay, W., *The Gospel of Luke* (Edinburgh: Saint Andrew Press, 1975).

Barrow, M., 'The Reason for the Seasons', *Primary Homework Help* (2013) http://www.primaryhomeworkhelp.co.uk/time/seasons.htm (accessed 18 April 2018).

Bass, D.C., *Receiving the Day* (Hoboken, NJ: Jossey-Bass, 2001).

Bock, D.L., *Luke*, The NIV Application Commentary (Grand Rapids, MI: Zondervan, 1996).

Borel, B., 'Do Plants Sleep?', *Popular Science* (2014) https://www.popsci.com/blog-network/our-modern-plagues/do-plants-sleep (accessed 27 July 2017).

Brain, P., *Going the Distance: How to Stay Fit for a Lifetime of Ministry* (Kingsford: Matthias Media, 2006).

Brueggemann, W., *Sabbath as Resistance: Saying No to the Culture of Now* (Louisville, KY: Westminster John Knox Press, 2014).

Buchanan, M., *The Rest of God* (Nashville, TN: Thomas Nelson, 2006).

Callard, F., Kimberley Staines, James Wilkes, eds. *The Restless Compendium* (Cham: Springer International Publishing, 2016).

Cosden, D., *The Heavenly Good of Earthly Work* (Milton Keynes: Paternoster, 2006).

Darton, K., *How to Manage Stress* (London: Mind, 2012).

Davies, G., *Stress: Sources and Solutions* (Fearn: Christian Focus Publications, 2005).

Davies, J., *God at Work: Creation Then and Now – A Practical Exploration* (Norwich: Canterbury Press, 2001).

Dawn, M.J., *Keeping the Sabbath Wholly: Ceasing, Resting, Embracing, Feasting* (Grand Rapids, MI: Eerdmans, 1989).

Dow, G., *A Christian Understanding of Daily Work* (Bramcote: Grove Books Ltd., 1994).

Dunn, J.D.G., *Jesus Remembered: Christianity in the Making* (Grand Rapids, MI: Eerdmans, 2003).

Enns, P., *Exodus*, The NIV Application Commentary (Grand Rapids, MI: Zondervan, 2000).

Feinberg, M., *Wonderstruck* (Brentwood, TN: Worthy Publishing, 2012).

Fretheim, T.E., *Exodus*, Interpretation commentary series (Louisville, KY: Westminster John Knox Press, 1991).

Goldingay, J., and R. Innes, *God at Work* (Bramcote: Grove Books Ltd., 1994).

Greig, P., *God on Mute: Engaging the Silence of Unanswered Prayer* (Eastbourne: Kingsway, 2007).

Green, R., *90,000 Hours: Managing the World of Work* (Bletchley: Scripture Union, 2002).

Grunfeld, D., *The Sabbath: A Guide to its Understanding and Observance* (Jerusalem: Feldheim Publishers, 1981).

Hagner, D.A., *Matthew 1–13*, Word Biblical Commentary (Dallas, TX: Word Books, 1993).

Hart, A., *The Hidden Link Between Adrenaline and Stress: The Exciting New Breakthrough That Helps You Overcome Stress Damage* (Nashville, TN: W. Publishing Group, 1995).

Heschel, A.J., *The Sabbath* (New York: Farrar, Straus and Giroux, 1951).

Horsfall, T., *Working from a Place of Rest: Jesus and the Key to Sustaining Ministry* (Abingdon: The Bible Reading Fellowship, 2010).

John, J., *Ten: Living the Ten Commandments in the 21st Century* (Eastbourne: Kingsway Communications Ltd., 2000).

Jukes, J., ed., *A Spirituality of Work* (London: Catholic Media, 2001).

MacDonald, G., *Ordering Your Private World* (Nashville, TN: Thomas Nelson, 2012).

McGeachy, C., *Spiritual Intelligence in the Workplace* (Dublin: Veritas Publications, 2001).

Meyers, R.R., *Saving Jesus from the Church: How to Stop Worshiping Christ and Start Following Jesus* (New York: HarperCollins, 2009).

Mignot, E., 'Why we sleep', *PLOS Biology*.

Miller, P.D., *The Ten Commandments*, Interpretation commentary series (Louisville, KY: John Knox Press, 2009).

Miller, S., *Rhythms of Rest: Finding the Spirit of Sabbath in a Busy World* (Minneapolis, MN: Bethany House, 2016).

Moltmann, J., *God in Creation: An Ecological Doctrine of Creation* (London: SCM Press Ltd., 1985).

Moo, D.J., 'Creation and New Creation: Transforming Christian Perspectives' in *Creation in Crisis: Christian Perspectives on Sustainability* (ed. Robert S. White; London: SPCK, 2009).

Murray, D., *Reset: Living a Grace-Paced Life in a Burnout Culture* (Wheaton, IL: Crossway, 2017).

Newell, J.P., *The Book of Creation: The Practice of Celtic Spirituality* (Norwich: Canterbury Press, 1999).

Nolland, J., *Luke 9:21 – 18:34*, Word Biblical Commentary (Dallas, TX: Word Books, 1993).

O'Rourke OSA, B., *Finding Your Hidden Treasure: The Way of Silent Prayer* (Liguori: Liguori Publications, 2010).

Peterson, E., *The Contemplative Pastor: Returning to the Art of Spiritual Direction* (Grand Rapids, MI: Eerdmans, 1989).

Rohr, R., *Simplicity: The Freedom of Letting Go* (New York: The Crossroad Publishing Company, 2004).

Rohr, R., *The Divine Dance* (London: SPCK, 2016).

Silf, M., *One Hundred Wisdom Stories from Around the World* (Oxford: Lion Publishing, 2003).

Smail, T., *Once and For All: A Confession of the Cross* (Eugene, OR: Wipf & Stock Publishers, 1998).

Stackhouse, I., *The Day is Yours* (Milton Keynes: Paternoster, 2014).

Tilby, A., *Let There Be Light: Praying with Genesis* (London: Darton, Longman & Todd, 2006).

Vanier, J., *Community and Growth* (London: Darton, Longman & Todd, 2007).

Vermes, G., *Jesus in the Jewish World* (London: SCM Press, 2010).

Walton, J.H., *Genesis*, The NIV Application Commentary (Grand Rapids, MI: Zondervan, 2001).

Wenham, G.I., *Genesis 1–15*, Word Biblical Commentary series (Nashville, TN: Thomas Nelson, 1987).

Wilkins, M.J., *Matthew*, The NIV Application Commentary (Grand Rapids, MI: Zondervan, 2004).

Wirzba, N., *From Nature to Creation: A Christian Vision for Understanding and Loving Our World* (Grand Rapids, MI: Baker Academic, 2015).

Wirzba, N., *Living the Sabbath: Discovering the Rhythms of Rest and Delight* (Grand Rapids, MI: Brazos Press, 2006).

Wright, T., *Matthew for Everyone: Part 1* (London: SPCK, 2002).

Wright, T., *Simply Jesus: Who He Was, What He Did, Why it Matters* (London: SPCK, 2011).

Zeitlin, I.M., *Jesus and the Judaism of His Time* (Cambridge: Polity Press, 1988).

Scripture Index

Subject Index

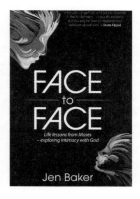

Face to Face

Life lessons from Moses –
exploring intimacy with God

Jen Baker

God longs for us to personally experience more of him, but so often we refuse or feel unable to draw close to him. Even the great hero of faith Moses hid his face from God, yet was eventually transformed into someone who spoke face to face with him.

Jen Baker explores Moses' life to see how he was able to move from hiddenness to holiness and encourages us to follow his example. Interwoven with personal testimony, Jen gently challenges and shows us how to move out of the shadows into the light of God's love.

Whether you feel distant from God or want to deepen your relationship with him, *Face to Face* will help encourage you to experience God in a new and powerful way.

978-1-78893-056-7

Authentic

We trust you enjoyed reading this book from Authentic. If you want to be informed of any new titles from this author and other releases you can sign up to the Authentic newsletter by scanning below:

Online:
authenticmedia.co.uk

Follow us: